WOMEN
of the BIBLE

52 Stories for
Prayer and Reflection

Ann Spangler

ZONDERVAN®

ZONDERVAN.com/
AUTHORTRACKER
follow your favorite authors

For information on Ann Spangler, visit www.annspangler.com.
If you would like to invite Ann to speak to your group,
contact her at annsdesk@annspangler.com.

BV4844
.S667
2002

0495 31477

ZONDERVAN

Women of the Bible: 52 Stories for Prayer and Reflection
Copyright © 1999, 2002 by Ann Spangler and Jean Syswerda
An abridgment of *Women of the Bible*
Copyright © 1999 by Ann Spangler and Jean Syswerda

Requests for information should be addressed to:

Zondervan, *Grand Rapids, Michigan* 49530

Library of Congress Cataloging-in-Publication Data

Spangler, Ann.
        Women of the Bible: 52 stories for prayer and reflection / Ann Spangler.
            p. cm.
        ISBN   978-0-310-24493-6
        1. Women—Prayer—books and devotions—English.   2. Devotional
        calendars. 3. Women in the Bible.   I. Title.
        BV4844 .S667 2002
        220.9'2'082—dc21

                                                                                2002004795

Published in association with the literary agency of Wolgemuth & Associates, Inc.

Interior design by Susan Ambs

Printed in the United States of America

---

10 11 12 13 14 • 28 27 26 25 24 23 22 21 20 19 18 17 16 15 14 13

TO JUDY WEAVER
Your faith has strengthened mine

CONTENTS

ALPHABETICAL INDEX OF WOMEN

INTRODUCTION

𝒯he Bible is so much more than a dry compilation of genealogies, prophecies, and laws. It is the story of the most important relationship in the world, the one between God and his people. The setting of this story moves quickly from Paradise to a fallen world and then culminates, after much foolishness and suffering, in heaven itself. It reveals what was, what is, and what will be. As the story unfolds, it exposes the nature of our deepest problems and the roots of our worst sufferings. Through its various characters, we recognize the tug-of-war that takes place in our own souls as we struggle to respond to God.

Sometimes the most profitable and enjoyable way to understand any historical era is to learn the stories of its most famous men and women, people whose lives both reflect and influence the times in which they lived. A popular television series, *Biography*, does just this. The series promotes itself with an intriguing tagline, assuring us that "Every Life Has a Story." The same could certainly be said of the women of the Bible, whose lives reveal so much about God's character and his strategy for saving us.

Though we are familiar with Adam, Abraham, Noah, Moses, Samson, Saul, David, and Peter—a few of the Bible's most noteworthy men—many of us would fail to recognize Hagar, Miriam, Deborah, Naomi, and Esther, to say nothing of Jael, Rizpah, or Joanna. We know how the men fit into the story of salvation, but what of the women? What do their stories tell us about God's love and our own response to him?

Women of the Bible looks at the lives of fifty-two prominent—and not so prominent—women of Scripture, telling the great story of salvation from their successive points of view. The cast of characters is long and colorful, including a parade of prostitutes, evil queens, prophetesses, wealthy women, abused women, single and married women, and widows young and old. Far from being one-dimensional characters, these are real women who struggled with tragedy and sometimes created it, who risked their lives and their reputations for the sake of others, whose compassion and wisdom often saved the day. Even though our culture is vastly different from theirs, we share many of their emotional responses and concerns. We agonize over infertility, worry about our children, long for a little affection, strive for wisdom, and sometimes harbor doubt about God's real intentions toward us. Their stories reveal so much about God's love, his relentless jealousy, and his creative ability to bring good out of the most desperate of circumstances.

Though I have sometimes added minor fictional elements to their stories to draw out a character's emotional responses, I have tried to remain as close as possible to the original text. The key Scriptures at the beginning of each woman's story contain the main Scripture passages that pertain to her life.

This edition represents an abridgment of a much larger work: *Women of the Bible: A One-Year Devotional Study of Women in Scripture*, which I coauthored with Jean Syswerda.

In addition to the debt I owe to Jean for her work on the original book, I owe a special debt of gratitude to my editors, Sandy Vander Zicht, for her insight, encouragement, and advocacy, and Rachel Boers, for her skilled and painstaking work on the manuscript of the original book, and Lori VandenBosch and Dirk Buursma, for their diligent attention to the details of this edition. I am also grateful to my agent, Robert Wolgemuth, and to Sue Brower and her creative marketing team for catching the vision for this book. Thanks also goes to Leanne Van Dyk for her insightful theological review and to George Martin for his careful biblical review and comments. Few books can succeed without champions, and I am grateful that these are some of mine.

Any deficiencies in the book, of course, can be traced only to me. Whatever they might be, I hope they do not prevent readers from gaining, as I have, a deeper appreciation for all the women of faith who have gone before us, living their lives in the light of God's presence.

—*Ann Spangler, April 2002*

1

EVE

Her Name Means "Life-giving"
or "Mother of All Who Have Life"

HER CHARACTER:	She came into the world perfectly at peace with her God and with her husband, the only other person on the planet. She lived in Paradise, possessing every pleasure imaginable. She never knew the meaning of embarrassment, misunderstanding, hurt, estrangement, envy, bitterness, grief, or guilt until she listened to her enemy and began to doubt God.
HER SORROW:	That she and her husband were banished from Paradise and the presence of God, and that her first son was a murderer and her second son his victim.
HER JOY:	That she had once tasted Paradise, and that God had promised her offspring would eventually destroy her enemy.
KEY SCRIPTURES:	Genesis 1:26–31; Genesis 2–4

The woman stirred and stretched, her skin soft and supple as a new-born's. One finger, then another moved in gentle exploration of the ground that gently cradled her. She felt warm and full, surrounded by a thousand joys at once. Then a sound she could not name tickled her throat and escaped her lips. Her body was shaking with a laughter she could not contain. And then a touch calmed her without diminishing her joy.

Her eyes opened to a Brightness, her ears to a Voice. And then a smaller voice, echoing an elated response: "This is now bone of my bones and flesh of my flesh; she shall be called 'woman,' for she was taken out of man." Adam took hold of her, and their laughter met like streams converging.

The man and the woman walked together naked and unashamed in Paradise, at ease with themselves and God. No shadows filled Eden, no disorder, discord, or fear.

One day a serpent spoke to the woman. "Did God really say, 'You must not eat from any tree in the garden'? You will not surely die. For God knows that when you eat of it your eyes will be opened, and you will be like God, knowing good and evil."

The woman listened. She remembered the Brightness, the Voice of God that had filled her with joy. Could she really be like God? Doubt and desire pursued her until she not only plucked and ate the fruit but also shared it with her husband. Suddenly, darkness rushed on Eden. It came, not from the outside but from inside, filling their souls with shadows and cravings. Order gave way to disorder, harmony to discord, trust to fear.

Soon Adam and Eve heard the sound of their Creator walking in the garden, and they hid. "Where are you, Adam?" God called.

"I heard you in the garden," Adam replied, "and I was afraid because I was naked, so I hid."

Sin had driven its wedge into their hearts, and God banished them from Eden, pronouncing judgment first on the wily serpent who had tempted the woman and then on her and her husband. To the serpent's curse he added this promise: "I will put enmity between you and the woman, and between your offspring and hers; he will crush your head, and you will strike his heel." To the woman, God said: "I will greatly increase your pains in childbearing; with pain you will give birth to children. Your desire will be for your husband, and he will rule over you."

Then God warned Adam: after a lifetime of hard labor, his strength would decrease until his body would finally be wrapped in the dust from which God had formed him. The curse of death fell suddenly upon the new world.

So Adam and his wife fled Paradise, and Adam named her Eve, because she would be the mother of all the living. But her firstborn, Cain, became a murderer, and her second son, Abel, his victim.

Sorrow upon sorrow entered the heart of the first woman, and the last we see of her we imagine her not as a creature springing fresh from God's hand, but as a woman in anguish. Her skin, damaged by sun and age, now stretches like worn canvas across her limbs. Her hands are restless spiders, clawing the hard ground beneath her, grasping for something to ease her pain. She can feel the child inside, filling her, his body pressing for a way of escape. The cries of mother and child meet like streams converging. And Seth is born.

With her child cradled against her breast, relief begins to spread across Eve's face. As she rests, a smile forms, and then, finally, laughter rushes from her lips. Try as she might, she can't stifle her joy. For she remembers the Brightness and the Voice and the promise God gave: sooner or later, despite many griefs, her seed would crush the serpent. The woman would win.

Her Legacy of Prayer

So God created man in his own image, in the image of God he created him; male and female he created them.

—*Genesis 1:27*

REFLECT ON: Genesis 2:15–25; 3.

PRAISE GOD: Because he created you in his own image, making you a woman capable of reflecting his love, truth, strength, goodness, wisdom, and beauty.

OFFER THANKS:	That embedded in God's judgment of Adam and Eve is the promise of a Redeemer who will crush the head of our enemy, the devil.
CONFESS:	Your own tendency to mar God's image in you by preferring your will to his.
ASK GOD:	To help you surrender your life, so that he can fulfill his purpose for creating you.

Lift Your Heart

*F*ind a peaceful setting, surrounded by the beauty of creation, to meditate on what life must have been like in the Garden of Eden. Think about what your life would be like if you experienced peace in all your relationships, if you never suffered physical or emotional pain, if you were never confused or ashamed or guilty, if you always experienced God's love and friendship. Let your imagination run riot as it fills in the details of God's original intention for your life and for those you love. Then consider this: You were made for paradise. The joys you taste now are infinitesimal compared to those that await you in heaven, for "no eye has seen, no ear has heard, no mind has conceived what God has prepared for those who love him" (1 Corinthians 2:9).

Father, give me a greater understanding of your original plan for our world. Help me to envision its beauty so I might live with a constant awareness that you intend to restore paradise to all who belong to you. May I surrender every sin and every sorrow to you, trusting that you will fulfill your purpose for my life.

— 2 —

SARAH
Her Name Means
"Chieftainness" or "Princess"

HER CHARACTER: Beautiful enough to attract rulers in the ancient world, she could be strong-willed and jealous. Yet Sarah was considered a loyal wife who did what was right and who didn't give in to fear.

HER SORROW: That she remained childless for most of her life.

HER JOY: That at the age of ninety, she gave birth to Isaac, child of the promise.

KEY SCRIPTURES: Genesis 12:1–20; 16:1–8; 17:1–22; 18:1–15; 21:1–13; Galatians 4:22–31

$\mathcal{V}$

$\mathcal{S}$arah was sixty-five, the age many of us retire, when she began a journey that would lead her into uncharted spiritual territory. Leaving behind their homeland, she and her husband, Abraham, moved hundreds of miles south to Canaan, a land fertile with the promises of God but barren of everything cherished and familiar. God had promised the land to Abraham and his offspring. From him would come not just a family, clan, or tribe but an entire nation, a people who would belong to God as no other people had.

The promise spread like ripples from a stone pitched in water. If Abraham was to father a new nation, surely Sarah would be its mother.

Yet she longed to give birth, not to a nation, but to one small child she could kiss and cradle.

At first Abraham and Sarah found it difficult to support themselves, let alone children, in their new homeland. Soon a famine made life so severe that they moved on to Egypt, where Abraham, fearful of Pharaoh, suggested a deceptive maneuver to save his skin: "I know what a beautiful woman you are. When the Egyptians see you, they will say, 'This is his wife.' Then they will kill me but will let you live. Say you are my sister [she was his half sister], so that I will be treated well for your sake and my life will be spared because of you."

So Sarah did as her husband asked and Pharaoh soon added her to his harem of beautiful women. For the privilege, he paid Abraham in the currency of the day—a bevy of sheep, cattle, donkeys, camels, and servants. But though the two men seemed satisfied with their bargain, God was not pleased, and proceeded to strike Pharaoh and his entire household with various diseases. The Egyptian ruler soon summoned Abraham, demanding an explanation. As soon as he heard the truth, he allowed both Sarah and Abraham to leave, taking with them all the riches they had gained in Egypt.

So the couple moved home again. By now, several years had passed since Abraham and Sarah had heard the remarkable promise of God, but still there was no child. So Sarah took matters into her own hands. Following a practice common in the ancient world, she gave Abraham permission to sleep with her Egyptian maid, Hagar. Sarah's slave would become a surrogate mother for the promised child.

Before long, Ishmael was born. But the child brought only discord between the two women.

One day the Lord appeared to Abraham while he was sitting at the entrance to his tent.

"Where is your wife, Sarah?"

"There in the tent," Abraham replied.

Then the Lord said, "I will surely return to you about this time next year, and Sarah, your wife, will have a son."

Now Sarah, who had been eavesdropping from inside the tent, laughed and said, "After I am worn out and my master is old will I now have this pleasure?"

But the Lord said to Abraham, "Why did Sarah laugh and say, 'Will I really have a child now that I am old?' Is anything too hard for the Lord? I will return to you at the appointed time next year and Sarah will have a son."

Because Sarah was afraid, she lied and said, "I did not laugh."

But he pressed her, saying, "Yes, you did laugh."

A year later, Sarah gave birth to Isaac, whose name meant "laughter." Of course the joke was not lost on the ninety-year-old mother, who exclaimed: "God has brought me laughter, and everyone who hears about this will laugh with me."

But Sarah's humor was short-lived. Fireworks flared once again between the two mothers until Sarah forced Hagar and Ishmael from Abraham's household, leaving them to wander in the harsh desert. And though God provided for the two outcasts, it would be through Isaac that he would keep his promise of a new nation and a deliverer for his people.

Sarah died at the age of 127 and was buried in Hebron. Between Isaac's birth and her own death lay thirty-seven years, ample time to reflect on her life's adventure with God. Was she ashamed of her treatment of the ill-fated Hagar? Did she remember laughing when God told Abraham she would bear a child at the age of ninety? Did she appreciate the echoing irony in young Isaac's laughter? Did she have any idea she would one day be revered as the Mother of Israel, indeed, a symbol of the promise just as Hagar was to become a symbol of slavery under the law? Scripture does not say. But it is heartening to realize that God accomplishes his purposes despite our frailties, our little faith, our entrenched self-reliance.

True, Sarah's pragmatic attempts to help God keep his promise caused plenty of anguish. (Even in our own day, the struggle between Israel and her Arab neighbors stems from the ancient strife between two women and the children they bore.) Still, despite her jealousy, anxiety, and skepticism about God's ability to keep his promises, there's no denying that Sarah was a risk-taker of the first order, a woman who said good-bye to everything familiar to travel to a land she knew nothing about. A real flesh-and-blood kind of lady who lived an adventure more strenuous than any fairy-tale heroine, an adventure that began with a promise and ended with laughter.

Her Legacy of Prayer

> God also said to Abraham, "As for Sarai your wife, you are no longer to call her Sarai; her name will be Sarah. I will bless her and will surely give you a son by her. I will bless her so that she will be the mother of nations; kings of peoples will come from her."
> —*Genesis 17:15–16*

REFLECT ON: Genesis 17:1–22.

PRAISE GOD: Because he keeps his promises.

OFFER THANKS: That God has a gracious plan for you that will unfold in his time, according to his way.

CONFESS: Your anxiety and self-reliance.

ASK GOD: To help you wait with a listening ear and a ready heart to do his will.

Lift Your Heart

God hints at his purpose for you by planting dreams within your heart. Sarah's dream was to give birth to a son. Find a quiet place and spend some time focusing on your dreams. Ask yourself what dreams you've been too busy, too afraid, or too disappointed to pursue. Write them down and pray about each one. God may be telling you to wait, or he may be giving you the go-ahead to pursue one in particular. If it's time to take the plunge, you might just find yourself joyfully echoing Sarah's words in Genesis 21:6: "God has brought me laughter."

Father, thank you for loving me despite the fact that my soul still contains shadows that sometimes block the light of your Spirit. As I grow older, may I trust you more completely for the dreams you've implanted in my soul, the promises you've made to me. Like Sarah, may I be surrounded by laughter at the wonderful way you accomplish your purpose despite my weakness.

— 3 —

HAGAR

Her Name Is Egyptian and
May Mean "Fugitive" or "Immigrant"

HER CHARACTER:	A foreigner and slave, she let pride overtake her when she became Abraham's wife. A lonely woman with few resources, she suffered harsh punishment for her mistake. She obeyed God's voice as soon as she heard it and was given a promise that her son would become the father of a great nation.
HER SORROW:	That she was taken from her homeland to become a slave in a foreign land where she was mistreated for many years.
HER JOY:	To know that God cared, that he saw her suffering and heard her cry, and that he helped her when she needed him most.
KEY SCRIPTURES:	Genesis 16; 21:8–21; Galatians 4:22–31

An Egyptian slave and Sarah's bitter rival, Hagar still had one thing going for her that her mistress never enjoyed: a personal revelation of God, who lovingly intervened on her behalf, not once but twice. It happened when she was alone and afraid, without a shekel to her name—but that's getting ahead of the story.

20

You may remember that Abraham, whom we honor as the father of faith, showed little evidence of that faith when he and Sarah first entered Egypt to escape a famine in Canaan. Certain the Egyptians would kill him once they caught sight of his beautiful wife, he advised her to pose as his sister. Soon enough, Pharaoh added Sarah to his harem and rewarded Abraham with an abundance of camels, sheep, cattle, donkeys, and servants. But God punished Pharaoh for his unwitting error so effectively that, when he found out that Sarah was actually Abraham's wife, he begged the two of them to leave Egypt with all their belongings. Possibly, Hagar was part of the booty Abraham and Sarah took with them—a gift that later backfired.

Still, of the three parties involved in the scheme to make Hagar a surrogate mother, she was perhaps the only innocent one, a slave with little power to resist. For Hagar to bear Abraham's heir, she had to become not just a concubine but a wife. But when Sarah raised Hagar to that position, she opened the door to spiritual catastrophe. As soon as Hagar discovered her pregnancy, she began lording it over her mistress—not a smart move for a young foreigner up against a woman entrenched in her husband's affections.

In fact, Sarah made life so difficult for Hagar that she fled into the desert, a desperate move for a young woman bearing a child so far from home. She hadn't gotten far before she heard a voice calling, "Hagar, servant of Sarah, where have you come from, and where are you going? Go back to your mistress and submit to her." But then, as if to sweeten the order, came a word of assurance: "You are now with child, and you will have a son. You shall name him Ishmael, for the Lord has heard of your misery."

Remarkably, Hagar didn't argue but turned right around and retraced her steps. God's word penetrated the wilderness of her heart like a fresh spring nourishing a desert oasis. Her bondage, her bitterness, her anxiety about the future—God had seen every bit of it. He knew about the child in her womb, naming him Ishmael, meaning "God hears." In the future, every time Hagar would hold her son close, watch him play, or worry about his future, she would remember that God was near, listening for the child's cry. Little wonder that she had responded to the voice in the desert by calling the Lord "the God who sees me."

Some sixteen years later, Hagar found herself once again in the wilderness, this time by force rather than by choice. In a crescendo of bitterness, Sarah had expelled her and Ishmael from their home. Dying from thirst, Hagar placed her son under a bush and withdrew, unable to witness his agony.

Her weeping was soon broken by an angel's voice. "Do not be afraid; God has heard the boy crying as he lies there. Lift the boy up and take him by the hand, for I will make him into a great nation." With that, the angel of the Lord opened Hagar's eyes so that she discovered a well of water nearby that would save her son's life. (The well became known as Beer Lahai Roi, or the "well of the Living One who sees me.")

The last we see of Hagar, she is living in the Desert of Paran in the Sinai Peninsula, busy securing a wife, and therefore a future, for Ishmael. God had made a way in the wilderness for a single woman and her son, without friends, family, or resources to help her. He had seen, he had heard, and he had indeed been faithful.

Her Legacy of Prayer

> *"What is the matter, Hagar? Do not be afraid; God has heard the boy crying as he lies there. Lift the boy up and take him by the hand, for I will make him into a great nation."*
>
> —*Genesis 21:17–18*

REFLECT ON: Genesis 21:8–21.

PRAISE GOD: Because he is an all-knowing Father who hears the cries of his children. Nothing that happens to us can ever escape his notice.

OFFER THANKS: That the Lord runs after the weak and the
                 helpless, to show them his mercy and his plan
                 of blessing for their lives.

CONFESS: Any pride, selfishness, or other sin that may
                 have contributed to your present circum-
                 stances.

ASK GOD: To open your eyes to the way he is providing
                 for and protecting you and your children. Ask
                 him to help you live each day, not as a slave to
                 the law but as a child of grace.

Lift Your Heart

*I*nvite a couple of close friends to share a Middle Eastern feast with olives, figs, pita bread, nuts, hummus, tabbouleh, and your favorite drink. Pray a special grace thanking God for providing so richly for you even when you felt you were living through a desert season in your life. Share stories with each other about how God has provided even when you weren't sure he was listening to your prayers.

Hummus

In a food processor blend 2 cups of cooked or canned chickpeas, drained, with 2/3 cup sesame paste (tahini), 3/4 cup lemon juice, salt and freshly ground pepper to taste, and 2 peeled garlic cloves. Stir in 1/4 cup finely chopped scallions. Makes about 3 cups. A great dip for bread, chips, or fresh vegetables.

Tabbouleh

1. Place 3/4 cup uncooked cracked wheat in a glass bowl and cover with cold water for 30 minutes; then drain completely. (For a softer texture, cover with boiling water and let stand for one hour before draining.)

2. Add 1 and 1/2 cups chopped fresh parsley; 3 medium tomatoes, chopped; 5 green onions, thinly sliced (with tops); and 2 tablespoons chopped fresh or 2 teaspoons crushed dried mint leaves.
3. In a separate bowl, mix 1/4 cup olive oil, 1/4 cup lemon juice, 3/4 teaspoon salt, and 1/4 teaspoon pepper. Pour over cracked wheat mixture and toss.
4. Cover and refrigerate at least one hour. Serve with a garnish of mint leaf. Makes 6 servings, about 3/4 cup each.

———————————

Lord, sometimes I feel abandoned, as though no one understands or cares about me. Please show me that you really are near, and that you see and hear everything that happens. Refresh me with your presence even when I am walking through a desert experience. And help me, in turn, to comfort others when they feel hopeless and alone.

4
LOT'S WIFE

HER CHARACTER:	She was a prosperous woman who may have been more attached to the good life than was good for her. Though there is no indication she participated in the sin of Sodom, her story implies she had learned to tolerate it and that her heart had become divided as a result.
HER TRAGEDY:	That her heart's choice led to judgment rather than mercy, and that she ultimately refused God's attempts to save her.
KEY SCRIPTURES:	Genesis 18:16–19:29; Luke 17:28–33

Lot's wife had only hours to live, though she never suspected it. She must have gone about her business as usual, tidying the house, cooking and kibitzing with the neighbors, unaware of the tragedy about to overtake her.

Years earlier she had married Abraham's nephew, and the two had amassed a fortune in land and livestock. Eventually, they settled in Sodom, uncomfortably comfortable in a city so wicked that heaven itself dispatched angels to investigate the allegations against it.

Lot, it so happened, was at the city gate at the very moment the angels arrived. Greeting the strangers, he quickly implored them to spend the night in his home, anxious about what might happen to them once night had fallen.

Lot's wife must have welcomed the strangers warmly too, for hospitality was a sacred trust in the ancient world. Then, just before bedtime, she would have heard the voices. At first a few muffled words and then echoing laughter and finally an ugly clamor as a noose of men tightened around the house. Rough voices shouted for her husband to open the door and surrender his guests to their pleasure.

"No, my friends. Don't do this wicked thing!" Lot screamed back. But the crowd was furious for its own way. Then he attempted an appalling bargain. "Look, I have two daughters who have never slept with a man. Let me bring them out to you, and you can do what you like with them. But don't do anything to these men, for they have come under the protection of my roof." But the men of Sodom would not be thwarted, and rushed the door to force their way in.

Suddenly, the angels reached out, pulled Lot back into the house, and struck the men at the door blind. Then they turned to Lot, urging him, "Do you have anyone else here—sons-in-law, sons or daughters, or anyone else in the city who belongs to you? Get them out of here, because we are going to destroy this place."

But Lot's sons-in-law thought he was joking and refused to leave.

At dawn the angels again urged Lot to hurry lest he and his wife and daughters perish with the rest of the city. Still, the family hesitated until the angels finally grabbed their hands and dragged them out, urging, "Flee for your lives! Don't look back, and don't stop anywhere in the plain! Flee to the mountains, or you will be swept away!"

By the time Lot and his family reached the small city of Zoar, the sun had risen over the land and everything in Sodom was engulfed in burning sulfur. Men, women, children, and livestock were all obliterated. A terrible judgment for terrible sin.

But the judgment was even worse than either Lot or his daughters first realized. Safe at last, they must have turned to each other in relief at their escape and then turned again in shock, realizing one of their number was missing. They would have searched, hoping against hope, until they finally caught sight of the white salt pillar, silhouetted against the sky, a lonely monument in the shape of a woman turning around toward Sodom.

If you have ever seen pictures of ancient Pompeii, destroyed by the eruption of Mount Vesuvius in A.D. 79, where human shapes are preserved to this day by the lava that stopped them dead in their tracks, you might imagine the disaster that overtook Lot's wife.

Why did she turn, despite the angel's clear warning? Was her heart still attached to everything she left behind in the city—a life of comfort, ease, and pleasure? Did she still have family trapped in the city? Or was she fascinated by the tragic spectacle taking place behind her, like a gawking motorist at the scene of a bloody accident? Perhaps all these things combined were a glue that caused her feet to slow, her head to turn, and her body to be overtaken by the punishment God had meant to spare her. By her own choice—her very last choice—she cast her lot with judgment rather than with mercy.

Jesus urged his followers to remember Lot's wife: "It will be just like this on the day the Son of Man is revealed. On that day no one who is on the roof of his house, with his goods inside, should go down to get them. Likewise, no one in the field should go back for anything. Remember Lot's wife! Whoever tries to keep his life will lose it, and whoever loses his life will preserve it" (Luke 17:30–33). Sobering words recalling a sobering story. Words meant to lead us away from the compelling illusions of wickedness and safe into the arms of mercy.

Her Legacy of Prayer

When he [Lot] hesitated, the men grasped his hand and the hands of his wife and of his two daughters and led them safely out of the city, for the LORD was merciful to them. As soon as they had brought them out, one of them said, "Flee for your lives! Don't look back, and don't stop anywhere in the plain!"

—Genesis 19:16–17

REFLECT ON: Genesis 19:1–26.

PRAISE GOD: That though he hates sin he also loves mercy.

OFFER THANKS: For ways that God has shown mercy to you
                  and members of your family.

CONFESS: Any tendency to ignore God's voice because
                  you prefer to go your own way.

ASK GOD: For the grace never to become rigid because
                  of your attachments or your sin.

Lift Your Heart

*I*n a society like ours, it's rare to find someone who isn't attached to creature comforts. Test your own level of attachment by taking a week-long retreat from television, newspapers, magazines, catalogs, and shopping malls. Instead, carve out a time and place in your home, even if it's only a few minutes in a small corner or a closet, for silent prayer and praise. Ask God to reveal any disordered attachments or rigidity that may have developed in your own spirit. Tell him you want to be a woman who is free and flexible enough to respond quickly to his direction.

Lord, you call me to live in the world without embracing the ways of the world. Help me to live in a way that preserves my freedom to follow you wherever and however you lead. If I should leave behind a monument, may it be a reminder to others of faith and not foolishness.

5

REBEKAH

Her Name Probably Means
"Loop" or "Tie"

HER CHARACTER:	Hard-working and generous, she possessed a faith so great that she left her home forever to marry a man she had never seen or met. Yet she played favorites with her sons and failed to trust God fully for the promise he had made.
HER SORROW:	That she was barren for the first twenty years of her married life, and that she never again set eyes on her favorite son, Jacob, after he fled from his brother Esau.
HER JOY:	That God had gone to extraordinary lengths to pursue her, to invite her to become part of his people and his promises.
KEY SCRIPTURES:	Genesis 24; 25:19–34; 26:1–28:1–9

The sun was dipping beyond the western rim of the sky as the young woman approached the well outside the town of Nahor, five hundred miles northeast of Canaan. It was women's work to fetch fresh water each evening, and Rebekah hoisted the brimming jug to her shoulder, welcoming its cooling touch against her skin.

As she turned to go, a stranger approached, asking for a drink. Obligingly, she offered to draw water for his camels as well. She noticed the look of surprised pleasure that flashed across his face. Ten camels could put away a lot of water, she knew. But had she overheard his whispered prayer just moments earlier, her astonishment would have exceeded his: "O Lord, God of my master Abraham, give me success today, and show kindness to my master Abraham. May it be that when I say to a girl, 'Please let down your jar that I may have a drink,' and she says, 'Drink, and I'll water your camels too'—let her be the one you have chosen for your servant Isaac."

A simple gesture. A generous response. A young woman's future altered in a moment's time. The man Rebekah encountered at the well, Abraham's servant, had embarked on a sacred mission—to find Isaac a wife from among Abraham's own people rather than from among the surrounding Canaanites. Like her great-aunt Sarah before her, Rebekah would make the journey south to embrace a future she could hardly glimpse. Betrothed to a man twice her age whose name meant "laughter," she felt a sudden giddiness rise inside her. The God of Abraham and Sarah was wooing her, calling her name and no other, offering a share in the promise. God was forging a new nation to be his own people.

Isaac was forty when he first set eyes on Rebekah. Perhaps his heart echoed the joy of that first man, "Here at last is bone of my bones and flesh of my flesh!" So Isaac and Rebekah entered the tent of his mother Sarah and made love. And the Bible says she comforted Isaac after the death of his mother.

Rebekah was beautiful and strong like Sarah, yet she bore no children for the first twenty years of her life together with Isaac. Would she suffer as Sarah did this curse of barrenness? Isaac prayed and God heard, giving her not one, but two sons who wrestled inside her womb. And God told her: "Two nations are in your womb, and two peoples from within you will be separated; one people will be stronger than the other, and the older will serve the younger."

During the delivery, Jacob's infant fingers grasped the heel of his brother Esau, as though striving for first position. Though second by birth, he was first in his mother's affections. But Isaac loved Esau best.

Years later, when Isaac was old and nearly blind, he summoned his firstborn, Esau. "Get your weapons—your quiver and bow—and go out to the open country to hunt some wild game for me. Prepare me the kind of tasty food I like and bring it to me to eat, so that I may give you my blessing before I die."

But the clever Rebekah had overheard, and called quickly to Jacob, suggesting a scheme to trick the blessing from Isaac. Disguised as Esau, Jacob presented himself to his father for the much-coveted blessing.

Isaac then blessed Jacob, thinking he was blessing Esau: "May nations serve you and peoples bow down to you. Be lord over your brothers, and may the sons of your mother bow down to you. May those who curse you be cursed and those who bless you be blessed."

The patriarch had stretched out his hand and passed the choicest blessing to his younger son, thus recalling the words spoken about the two children jostling for position in Rebekah's womb. The benediction thus given could not be withdrawn, despite the deceit, despite Esau's tears, and despite his vow to kill Jacob.

Afraid of Esau's revenge, Rebekah persuaded Isaac to send Jacob to Haran to find a wife from among her brother Laban's daughters. She would send for Jacob as soon as his brother's fury abated.

Over the years, Rebekah must have pined for Jacob, praying for a chance to hold him close once more, to be given the privilege of enfolding his children in her embrace. But more than twenty years would pass before Jacob returned. And though Isaac would live to welcome his son, Rebekah would not.

As a young girl, God had invited Rebekah to play a vital role in the story of his people. He had gone to great lengths to pursue her. Like Sarah, she would become a matriarch of God's people, and like Sarah, her heart would divide itself between faith and doubt, believing that God's promise required her intervention. Finding it difficult to rest in God's promise to her, she resorted to trickery to achieve it. The results, mirroring her own heart, were mixed. Jacob indeed became heir to the promise, but he was driven from his home and the mother who loved him too well. In addition, he and his descendants would forever be at odds with Esau and his people, the Edomites. Two thousand years later, Herod the Great, a man of power who hailed from Idumea (the Greek and Roman name for Edom), would slaughter innocent children in his attempt to destroy the infant Jesus.

Yet God was still at work, graciously using a woman whose response to him was far less than perfect, to accomplish his purposes.

Her Legacy of Prayer

> *"Our sister, may you increase to thousands upon thousands; may your offspring possess the gates of their enemies."*
>
> —*Genesis 24:60*

REFLECT ON: Genesis 27.

PRAISE GOD: Because unlike Isaac, who had only one bless-
                  ing to give his children, God has blessings
                  uniquely designed for each of us.

OFFER THANKS: That God doesn't wait until we're perfect to
                  involve us in his plans.

CONFESS: Your tendency to try to control the future,
                  rather than trusting God to shape it according
                  to his timetable.

ASK GOD: To protect you from playing favorites with
                  your own children and to trust that he has a
                  generous plan for each one.

Lift Your Heart

Take a few minutes this week to write a blessing card for each of your children. Use a simple index card or decorate the card with stickers, stencils, or line drawings. (If you don't have children of your own, you can do this for a niece or nephew or another special child in your life.) Start by praying for each child, asking God's blessing on their lives. Then write out the blessings you sense God wants for them. Tuck the blessing cards under their pillows or place them next to their dinner plates. Tell them these are some of the ways you are asking God to bless them. Be sure to keep a copy of each card for yourself so you can make those blessings a subject of frequent prayer.

———————————

Lord, you give us the power to bless our children, through our example, our teaching, our love, and our prayers. May our children surpass us in faith. In all their struggles may they sense your nearness, and may their joy be renewed each morning. May each of them become the kind of person that attracts others to you.

6

RACHEL
Her Name Means "Ewe"

HER CHARACTER:	Manipulated by her father, she had little say over her own life circumstances and relationships. But rather than dealing creatively with a difficult situation, she behaved like a perpetual victim, responding to sin with yet more sin, making things worse by competing with her sister and deceiving her father in return.
HER TRAGEDY:	That her longing for children ultimately led to her death in childbirth.
HER JOY:	That her husband cherished her and would do whatever was in his power to make her happy.
KEY SCRIPTURES:	Genesis 29–35; Jeremiah 31:15; Matthew 2:18

"Was it better to have love but no children or to be unloved and yet mother to a house full of sons?" The question battered Rachel like a strong wind slamming the same door again and again.

Leah had just given birth to her fourth son, Judah. In her joy she had shouted, "I will praise the Lord!" Her firstborn, Reuben, meant "see, a son," Simeon, "one who hears," and Levi, "attached," as though Jacob could ever be attached to his plain wife! Rachel was sick to death of this habit her sister had of naming her sons in ways that emphasized Rachel's own barrenness.

Leah had snared Jacob through her father's treachery, but Rachel had captured his love from their first meeting at the well outside Haran. Every touch communicated his favor. Yet favor could not make children any more than wishing could make wealth. Rachel should have been his first, his only wife, just as Aunt Rebekah was Uncle Isaac's only wife.

Rachel's father, Laban, had promised her to his nephew, Jacob, provided he work for him for seven years. Seven years was a long time to wait for a wife, yet Jacob had thought it a good bargain. And that made Rachel love him all the more.

But as the wedding day approached, Laban hatched a scheme to trick seven more years of labor out of Jacob. Rachel's day of happiness dissolved the moment Laban instructed her older sister Leah to disguise herself in Rachel's wedding garments.

After dark he led Leah, veiled, to Jacob's tent, and the two slept together as man and wife. As the first light crept across the tent floor, Jacob reached again for Rachel only to find Leah at his side. Despite the deceit, despite the recriminations and the tears, the marriage could not be undone.

But Rachel felt undone, her blessing seized by stealth. Laban's convoluted plan, however, was still unfolding. He struck another bargain, giving Rachel to Jacob the very next week in exchange for seven more years of labor. So now the two sisters lived uneasily together, Leah's sons a grating reminder that Rachel, the second wife, was cheated still.

"Give me children or I'll die," she screamed at Jacob one day—as though he could take the place of God and open her womb. So she gave him Bilhah, her maid, who conceived and bore her two sons. When Napthali, the second son, was born, Rachel proclaimed to anyone who would listen, "I have had a great struggle with my sister, and I have won." But the wrestling match between Rachel and Leah was far from over.

Rachel's bitterness again eased when she herself gave birth to a son, naming him Joseph, meaning "may he add"—a prophetic prayer that God would add yet another child to her line.

Then one day God spoke to Jacob, telling him to return to the land of Isaac, his father. More than twenty years before, Jacob had wrestled the blessing from Esau and had fled his murderous wrath. Had the long years paid him back twofold? Had Laban's treachery since then and the wrestling match between Rachel and Leah reminded him of his own struggles with his brother? Would God—and Esau—call it even? Only the Lord could protect him in this matter with his brother.

As Jacob gathered his flocks, his servants, and his children, preparing to leave, Rachel stole her father's household gods, small idols thought to ensure prosperity. After ten days on the road, Laban overtook them in the hill country of Gilead, accusing his son-in-law of theft. Unaware of Rachel's deceit, Jacob invited Laban to search the camp, promising to put to death anyone discovered with the idols.

Having learned a trick or two from her crafty father, Rachel tucked the idols into a saddle and then sat on it. When Laban entered her tent, she greeted him with a woman's ruse, saying, "Don't be angry, my lord, that I cannot stand up in your presence; I'm having my period." Her trick worked, much as Jacob's had when he deceived his own father, and Laban finally gave up the search. Later, Jacob made sure that all the old idols were purged from his household.

As they made their way across the desert, Jacob faced his brother Esau, and the two reconciled. But tragedy soon overtook them as Rachel struggled to give birth to a second son, the answer to her many prayers. Ironically, the woman who once said she would die unless she had children was now dying because of a child. Rachel's last words, "He is Ben-Oni, the son of my trouble," capture her anguish at the birth of this son.

But Jacob gathered the infant in his arms and with a father's tenderness renamed him Benjamin, "son of my right hand." Like her husband, the beautiful Rachel had been both a schemer and the victim of schemes. Tricked by her own father, she viewed her children as weapons in the struggle with her sister. As so often happens, the lessons of treachery and competition were passed from generation to generation. Rachel's own son, Joseph, would suffer grievously as a result, being sold into slavery by his half brothers, Leah's sons.

Yet God would remain faithful. Through a remarkable set of twists and turns, Rachel's Joseph would one day rule Egypt, providing a refuge for his father and brothers in the midst of famine. Step by step, in ways impossible to foresee, God's plan was unfolding, a plan to heal divisions, put an end to striving, and restore hope. Using people with mixed motives and confused desires (the only kind of people there are), he was revealing his grace and mercy, never once forsaking his promise.

Her Legacy of Prayer

Then God remembered Rachel; he listened to her and opened her womb.
—*Genesis 30:22*

REFLECT ON: Genesis 30:1–24.

PRAISE GOD: Because he never for a moment forgets about us. He is present and attentive, aware of our deepest desires, even when we're certain he's lost track of us.

OFFER THANKS: That God alone is the Creator. Because of him, every human life is sacred.

CONFESS: That we sometimes use our children, our husbands, our homes, or even the size of our paychecks to compete with other women.

ASK GOD: To help you form deep and loyal friendships with other women so you can know the joy that comes from being sisters in Christ.

Lift Your Heart

Think of one woman you would like to get to know better in the next few months. Then pick up the phone and make a lunch date, or invite her to a play, movie, or concert. Make sure you build in a little time to chat so you can begin to build a relationship. One expert says it takes an average of three years to form a solid friendship. Don't waste another moment!

———————————

Father, forgive me for letting my identity rest on whose wife or mother I am or what kind of job I have. I don't want to view other women as my rivals but as potential friends and even soul mates. Please lead me to the friendships I desire, and help me to be patient with the process.

7

LEAH

Her Name May Mean
"Impatient" or "Wild Cow"

HER CHARACTER:	Capable of both strong and enduring love, she was a faithful mother and wife. Manipulated by her father, she became jealous of her sister, with whom, it seems, she never reconciled.
HER SORROW:	That she lacked her sister's beauty, and that her love for her husband was one-sided.
HER JOY:	That she bore Jacob six sons and one daughter.
KEY SCRIPTURES:	Genesis 29–35; Ruth 4:11

We buried Rachel today. But she is still alive. I catch glimpses of her yet in Jacob's broken heart, in dark-eyed Joseph and in squalling little Benjamin, his favorite sons. Rachel's sons. I can hear my beautiful, determined sister weeping loudly for the children she might have had, stubbornly refusing to be comforted. Yet who takes note of my tears? Should they flood the desert, no one would notice.

Reuben, Simeon, Levi, Judah, Issachar, Zebulun, Dinah, and then Gad and Asher by my maid—these are the children God has given me and I have given my beloved Jacob. And still he loves her best. Should my husband and I live another hundred years, I will never be his only wife.

Contrary to what Leah might have felt, God had taken note of her sorrow. Knowing well that Jacob's heart was too cramped a space to harbor both Rachel and Leah, he made Leah a mother, not once, but seven times, extending her influence in Jacob's household.

With each child the unhappy Leah hoped to secure her husband's affection. But each time her disappointment grew. She felt the old curse asserting itself: "Your desire will be for your husband and he will rule over you" (Genesis 3:16).

Perhaps Jacob still resented Leah for tricking him on their wedding night, disguising herself as his beloved Rachel. Surely Leah's love had been passionate enough to deceive him until morning. She felt both glad and guilty for her part; though, truth to tell, she had little choice but to obey her father, Laban, in the matter. And she thanked God each day for enabling her to bear Jacob's children. Still, children often caused a mother untold sorrow.

Dinah, her only daughter, had been raped by a local prince on their return to Jacob's homeland. Leah hardly knew how to comfort her. To make matters worse, her sons Levi and Simeon avenged their sister by savagely murdering a town full of people. Then Reuben disgraced himself by sleeping with his father's concubine Bilhah.

Hadn't God promised to protect them if they returned to this land of promise? How, then, could such things happen? Leah wondered. True, God had watched over them as they faced Esau and his four hundred men. But Leah's joy at the brothers' friendly reunion was eclipsed by her sorrow at once again being proved the lesser-loved wife. Jacob had made it plain enough by placing Rachel and her children last in their long caravan, giving them the best chance of escape should Esau turn violent.

But Jacob's love could not prevent Rachel from dying in childbirth. Leah, not Rachel, was destined to be his first and last wife. Alongside her husband, the father of Israel, she would be revered as a mother of Israel. In fact, the promise of a Savior was carried not through Rachel's Joseph but through Leah's Judah, whose descendants would include David, Israel's great king, and Jesus, the long-awaited Messiah. In the end, Jacob was laid to rest in the Cave of Machpelah, next to his first wife, Leah, rather than his favorite wife, Rachel, who was buried some-where near Ephrath.

The two sisters, Rachel and Leah, remind us that life is fraught with sorrow and peril, much of it caused by sin and selfishness. Both women suffered—each in her own way—the curse of Eve after she was expelled from her garden paradise. While Rachel experienced great pain in giving birth to children, Leah experienced the anguish of lov-ing a man who seemed indifferent to her. Yet both women became mothers in Israel, leaving their homeland to play essential roles in the story of God's great plan for his people.

Her Legacy of Prayer

When the LORD saw that Leah was not loved, he opened her womb, but Rachel was barren. Leah became pregnant and gave birth to a son. She named him Reuben, for she said, "It is because the LORD has seen my misery. Surely my husband will love me now."
—Genesis 29:31–32

REFLECT ON:	Genesis 29:16–31.
PRAISE GOD:	That though human beings often judge by outward appearances, God always sees the heart and judges accordingly.
OFFER THANKS:	That God is moved by our sorrow.
CONFESS:	Your tendency to compare yourself with other women, judging them and yourself merely by appearances.
ASK GOD:	To enable you to base your identity on your relationship with him rather than on what you see in the mirror.

Lift Your Heart

Take five minutes a day this week to pay yourself a compliment by thanking God for making you the woman you are. Call to mind everything you like about yourself—your quirky sense of humor, your love of great literature, your compassion for other people, your curly hair, even the shape of your toes. Resist the temptation to think about what you don't like. (Imagine for a moment how God must feel when he hears us complaining about how he has made us!) Instead, decide now to honor him by your gratitude. At the end of the week, treat yourself to lunch with a friend or a leisurely latte at your favorite café in celebration of all the natural gifts with which God has blessed you.

Lord, I don't want to be critical of how you've put me together, relying on what others think of me for my sense of well-being. Make me a woman who is confident that I am lovable, not because of any outward beauty but because you have loved me from the moment you called me into being.

— 8 —

TAMAR, DAUGHTER-IN-LAW OF JUDAH

Her Name Means "Date Tree" or "Palm Tree"

HER CHARACTER:	Driven by one overwhelming need, she sacrificed her reputation and nearly her life to achieve her goals.
HER SORROW:	That the men in her life failed to fulfill their responsibility, leaving her a childless widow.
HER JOY:	That her daring behavior resulted, not in ruin, but in the fulfillment of her hopes to bear children.
KEY SCRIPTURES:	Genesis 38; Matthew 1:3

γ

$\mathcal{G}$enealogies hardly make compelling reading at bedtime—or at any other time for that matter. Perhaps you welcome them with a yawn, or skip over them entirely as you read through the Bible. But even long lists of bewildering names can reveal interesting insights into God's mysterious plan. That's the way the Scriptures work, yielding hidden riches on every page.

Take the genealogy in the first chapter of Matthew, for instance. It lists a grand total of forty-one male ancestors of Jesus, beginning with Abraham, and a mere five female ancestors, three of whose stories (those of Tamar, Rahab, and Bathsheba) are colored by such distasteful details as incest, prostitution, fornication, and murder.

Jesus, the perfect Son of the perfect Father, had plenty of imperfect branches in his family tree and enough colorful characters to populate a modern romance novel. That women should be mentioned at all in his genealogy is surprising, let alone that four of the five got pregnant out of wedlock. In addition, four of the women were foreigners, not Israelites.

Tamar fell into both categories. Her father-in-law, Judah (son of Jacob and Leah), had arranged for her to marry his firstborn, Er. Half Canaanite and half Hebrew, Er was a wicked man, whom God killed for his sins. That's all we know of him.

After Er came Onan, Judah's second son. As was the custom of the time, Judah gave Onan to the widowed Tamar, instructing him to sleep with her so that she could have children to carry on Er's line. But Onan was too crafty for his own good. He slept with Tamar, but then spilled his semen on the ground, thus ensuring Tamar's barrenness. That way he would not be saddled with responsibility for children who would carry on his brother's line rather than his own. But God took note, and Onan, too, died for his wickedness.

Already Judah had lost two sons to Tamar. Should he risk a third? Shelah was his only remaining son, not yet fully grown. To placate his daughter-in-law, Judah instructed Tamar to return to her father's house and live as a widow until Shelah was of marriageable age. But time passed like a sluggish river, and Tamar continued to wear her widow's garments.

After Judah's wife died, he set out one day for Timnah to shear his sheep. Hearing the news of her father-in-law's journey, Tamar decided to take desperate and dramatic action. If Judah would not give his youngest son in marriage, she would do her best to propagate the family name in her own way. Shedding her widow's black, she disguised herself in a veil, impersonating a prostitute, and sat down beside the road to Timnah. When Judah came along, he slept with her and gave her his personal seal and cord along with his staff in pledge of future payment.

About three months later, Judah learned that Tamar was pregnant, little realizing he was responsible for her condition. Outraged that she had prostituted herself, he ordered her burned to death. But before the sentence could be carried out, Tamar sent him a stunning message: "I am pregnant by the man who owns these. See if you recognize whose seal and cord and staff these are."

The man who had so quickly passed judgment, little heeding his own secret tryst with a prostitute, was suddenly taken up short. To his credit, he told the truth, saying, "She is more righteous than I, since I wouldn't give her to my son Shelah."

Six months later, Tamar gave birth to twins. Once again, as with Jacob and Esau, the children struggled in her womb. A tiny hand came out and then disappeared, but not before being tied with a scarlet thread by the midwife. Then a small, slippery body emerged, but with no trace of the red thread. They named the first boy Perez (meaning "breaking out"). Then the little one with the scarlet ribbon was born and they named him Zerah (meaning "scarlet"). Perez was recognized as the firstborn. From his line would come King David and finally, hundreds of years later, Jesus of Nazareth.

Judah had shown little concern regarding the continuance of his line. Instead, God used a woman, shamed by her own barrenness and determined to overcome it, to ensure that the tribe of Judah would not only survive but that it would one day bear the world's Messiah.

Her Legacy of Prayer

Judah [was] the father of Perez and Zerah, whose mother was Tamar.
—from the genealogy of Christ in Matthew 1:3

REFLECT ON: Genesis 38.

PRAISE GOD: That he allowed his own Son to be intimately linked with fallen human beings from whom he was descended.

OFFER THANKS:	That God can use everyone and everything to bring about a good result.
CONFESS:	Any tendency you may have to judge others with a double standard, as Judah did Tamar.
ASK GOD:	To take any desperation you may be feeling and replace it with hope, calling to mind the verse in Jeremiah 29:11: "'For I know the plans I have for you,' declares the Lord, 'plans to prosper you and not to harm you, plans to give you hope and a future.'"

Lift Your Heart

*I*f you've never sketched out your family tree, make an effort to trace your heritage, going back at least four or five generations—more if you have the time and energy. Ask older relatives to supply as much information as possible about your ancestors. Pay special attention to the women in your family tree. Take notes on everything you discover. Then transcribe all the information into a keepsake book that can be passed along to your own children after you're gone. Include any photos and news clippings you can find. You may discover some fascinating insights into your family background.

Lord, you formed me in my mother's womb. You knew then what every single day of my life would be like. You saw the great things and the hard things, the joy and the sorrow. Right now I come before you with a situation [or a memory] with which I have not yet made peace. As I look back at painful circumstances, help me to realize that you were present even in the midst of them. And now, as I surrender them to you, help me to sense your healing presence in my life.

9

POTIPHAR'S WIFE

HER CHARACTER:	The wife of a prosperous and influential Egyptian, she was unfaithful and vindictive, ready to lie in order to protect herself and ruin an innocent man.
HER SORROW:	To be rebuffed by a slave.
KEY SCRIPTURE:	Genesis 39

We don't even know her name. She is merely presented as the spoiled wife of a prosperous Egyptian official, a miniature Cleopatra, determined to employ her charms to seduce the handsome young Hebrew slave, Joseph.

At the age of seventeen, Joseph was sold into slavery by his half brothers, the sons of Leah. The favorite child of Rachel and Jacob, Joseph seems to have unwittingly done everything possible to ensure his brothers' enmity, even recounting a dream predicting that he, the younger son, would one day rule over them. Envious, the brothers faked Joseph's death and contemptuously sold him to Midianite traders en route to Egypt.

There, Potiphar, captain of Pharaoh's executioners, bought the young slave and gradually entrusted him with responsibility for his entire household. Even in his exile, everything Joseph touched prospered, as Potiphar couldn't help but notice.

But the captain of the guard wasn't the only Egyptian impressed by Joseph. His wife had taken special note as well. She made her desire plain enough by inviting Joseph to share her bed. The young slave must have surprised his wealthy mistress with his quick rebuff: "My master has withheld nothing from me except you, because you are his wife. How then could I do such a wicked thing and sin against God?"

From then on, Joseph did his best to avoid her. But with little else to occupy her time and attention, Potiphar's wife simply waited for her next opportunity, which came when Joseph entered the house one day to attend to his duties. Alone with him, she caught hold of his cloak, whispering once again, "Come to bed with me!" But Joseph could not be persuaded and instead fled from her, leaving his would-be seducer alone with her lust, furiously clutching his cloak in her fingers.

Fearing, perhaps, that Joseph would speak to Potiphar about what had happened, she wasted no time accusing him of attempted rape. When her husband heard the news, he was outraged, quickly consigning his favorite servant to prison.

The story of Joseph and how God blessed him even in his prison cell, eventually enabling him to become master of the nation he had entered as a slave, is well-known to us. But we haven't a clue about Potiphar's wife. Whatever became of her? Did her husband suspect her duplicity? Is that why he merely confined Joseph to prison rather than executing him, as he had every right to do? Compared with Joseph, the story's protagonist, Potiphar's wife was a hollow woman whose soul was steadily decaying through the corrosive power of lust and hate. Surrounded by luxury, she was spiritually impoverished. Empty of God, she was full of herself.

Her Legacy of Prayer

Create in me a pure heart, O God, and renew a steadfast spirit within me.
—*Psalm 51:10*

REFLECT ON: Genesis 39.

PRAISE GOD: Because he not only shows us what is right, but he gives us the strength to resist temptation.

OFFER THANKS:	That he invites us to enjoy an intimate relationship with himself rather than the empty pleasures this world offers.
CONFESS:	Any tendency toward becoming emotionally or physically involved in an off-limits relationship or any tendency to covet what does not belong to you.
ASK GOD:	To help you break the habit of fantasizing about relationships you wish you had.

Lift Your Heart

We know what happened to Joseph after he was falsely accused, but we don't know anything about Potiphar's wife. Write a short account from your own imagination, titled "Whatever Became of Potiphar's Wife?" You can give her a happy ending or a sad one; just make sure it's believable. Try to put yourself in the story. You could be Potiphar's wife, her mother, her maid, her little sister, or whatever character you dream up. Does anything hit you as you ponder her story's conclusion?

Lord, I don't want my soul to feed on empty pleasures, to long for what belongs to someone else. Instead, increase my hunger for you and create in me a pure heart, one that you will find irresistibly beautiful.

10

THE MOTHERS
OF MOSES

JOCHEBED
Her Name Means "The Lord Is Glory"

HER CHARACTER: Her fierce love for her son, coupled with her faith, enabled her to act heroically in the midst of great oppression.

HER SORROW: To live in bondage as a slave.

HER JOY: That God not only preserved the son she surrendered to him but that he restored her child to her.

KEY SCRIPTURES: Exodus 2:1–10; Hebrews 11:23

PHARAOH'S
DAUGHTER

HER CHARACTER: The Jewish people honor men and women whom they designate as "righteous Gentiles." These are people who have assisted the Jewish people in some significant way. Surely,

Pharaoh's daughter should top the list of righteous Gentiles, courageously and compassion-
ately delivering a child from death, a child who
would one day act as Israel's great deliverer.

HER SORROW: That her adopted son eventually had to flee
his home in Egypt in order to escape
Pharaoh's wrath.

KEY SCRIPTURE: Exodus 2:1–10

Three hundred years after the death of the patriarch Joseph, a baby
boy was born in Egypt, his lusty cries muffled by a woman's sobs.
Jochebed's heart was a tangle of joy and fear. This son, his fingers forming a tiny fist against her breast, was so striking a child she hardly
believed he was hers. Tenderly she raised the small hand to her mouth,
pressing its warmth to her lips. Her gesture calmed them both. She
could feel the stiffness in her back dissolving, her muscles relaxing as
she watched the night shadows evaporate in the morning's light.

Slave though she was, she was yet a Levite, a woman who belonged
to the God of Abraham and Sarah, of Isaac and Rebekah, of Jacob,
Rachel, and Leah. She knew the stories. She believed the promises. God
was faithful. Hadn't her people already grown as numerous as the sand
of the sea, just as he said they would?

In fact, the Israelites were so numerous that the pharaohs feared they
might one day welcome an invading army and betray the nation from
within. Over time, the Egyptians had tightened their grip, finally enslaving the Israelites, until Pharaoh's paranoia produced an even greater
evil—a command to murder each Hebrew male child emerging from
the womb. But the Hebrew midwives feared God more than the king
and refused to follow his orders, excusing themselves by claiming that

Hebrew women were stronger than Egyptian women, giving birth before the midwives even arrived.

So Pharaoh commanded his soldiers to search out and smother every newborn male in the waters of the Nile. Jochebed could hear the screams of the mothers echoing regularly across the Hebrew camp as their children were torn from them. Her arms tightened around her own child as he slept quietly against her breast. This one, she vowed, would never be fodder for the Egyptian river god. She and her husband, Amram, would pray. They would plan. And they would trust God to help them.

For three months, as long as she dared, she hid the infant, managing to keep Miriam and three-year-old Aaron quiet about their new baby brother. Finally, she acted on an idea that had been growing in her mind. Pharaoh had commanded her to consign her son to the Nile River. All right then. Her own hands would put him into the water.

Remembering how God had spared the child Isaac, she bent down and laid her son in a basket of papyrus, waterproofed with tar and pitch. Then, with a whispered prayer and a last caress, she wiped her eyes, begging God to preserve her baby from the crocodiles that swarmed the river.

She could not bear to watch as the child drifted away from her. Instead, young Miriam kept vigil, following at a distance to see what would become of him. Soon Pharaoh's daughter arrived at the riverbank with some of her attendants. Spotting the basket among the reeds, she sent her slave girl to fetch it. As soon as she beheld the brown-eyed baby, she loved him. The river had brought her a child whom she would cherish as her own. She could not save all the innocent children, but she could spare one mother's son.

Was she surprised when a young slave girl, Miriam, approached, asking whether she could go after a Hebrew woman to nurse the baby for her? Did she suspect the truth when Jochebed gathered the boy in her arms, this time as his nursemaid?

Whatever was in her mind, she named the child Moses, saying, "I drew him out of the water." For the next forty years, Moses was educated as a prince in the courts of Pharaoh.

God kept Moses safe in the very midst of extraordinary evil and danger—first in crocodile-infested waters and then right under Pharaoh's nose. Ironically, he used the Egyptians to protect and educate him in ways that must have made Moses even more effective in his role as his people's deliverer.

Year after year, Jochebed would surely have reflected on the marvelous faithfulness of God. Her ingenuity, courage, and faith should inspire even the most weak-kneed among us.

Two women—a slave and a princess—preserved the life of Israel's future deliverer and so preserved the entire Jewish race.

Their Legacy of Prayer

When she could hide him no longer, she got a papyrus basket for him and coated it with tar and pitch. Then she placed the child in it and put it among the reeds along the bank of the Nile.

—*Exodus 2:3*

REFLECT ON: Exodus 2:1–10.

PRAISE GOD: That even the worst enemies we encounter
                  are weak compared to him.

OFFER THANKS: For God's power to save.

CONFESS: Any failure to trust God with the lives of our
                  children.

ASK GOD: To help you be an encouragement to another
                  mother who is concerned about her children's
                  well-being.

Lift Your Heart

*F*ind another mother, perhaps a teenage mom or a friend who is having difficulty with her own children right now. Put together a gift basket for her, filled with small gifts like a scented candle, dried fruit, a humorous mug, and some small cards inscribed with encouraging Scripture verses. Tell her you will be praying for each of her children by name every day for the next couple of months. Don't expect her to confide in you, but if she does, cherish what she tells you by keeping it confidential and letting it shape your prayers.

Father, thank you for the gift and calling of motherhood. Help me to remember that my love for my children is merely a reflection of your own love for them. With that in mind, give me grace to surrender my anxiety. Replace it with a sense of trust and calm as I learn to depend on you for everything.

11

MIRIAM

Her Name May Mean "Bitterness"

HER CHARACTER:	Even as a young girl, she showed fortitude and wisdom. A leader of God's people at a crucial moment in history, she led the celebration after crossing the Red Sea and spoke God's word to his people, sharing their forty-year journey through the wilderness.
HER SORROW:	That she was struck with a terrible skin disease for her pride and insubordination and was denied entry into the Promised Land.
HER JOY:	To have played an instrumental role in the deliverance of God's people, a nation she loved.
KEY SCRIPTURES:	Exodus 2:1–10; 15:20–21; Numbers 12:1–15

Seven days, I must stay outside the camp of my people, an old woman, fenced in by memories of what has been.

How could I forget our years in Egypt, the cries of the mothers whose children were murdered or the moans of our brothers as they worked themselves to death? I have only to shut my eyes and see—the wall of water, the soldiers chasing us through the sea, the sounds of their drowning, and, finally, the silence and the peace. How I miss the singing of the women I led that day, dancing at the sea's edge, praising God for hurling our enemies into the deep waters, certain we would never see them again.

But we did see them again—our enemies, though not the Egyptians. Ingratitude stalked us. Fear kept us from entering the land of promise.

Time and again Moses and Aaron and I exhorted the people to stand firm, to have faith, to obey God. But there came a day when Aaron and I could stand with our brother no longer. Instead we spoke against him and his Cushite wife. What part did she, a foreigner to our suffering, have in the promise? So we challenged Moses. Had the Lord spoken only through him? All Israel knew better. We deserved an equal share in his authority, an equal say in how to lead the people.

But the Lord who speaks also heard our complaint and summoned the three of us to stand before him at the Tent of Meeting. He addressed Aaron and me with terrible words.

When the cloud of his presence finally lifted, I was a leper. I could see the horror on every face. Aaron begged Moses to forgive us both. And Moses cried out to the Lord to heal me.

The Lord replied, "If her father had spit in her face, would she not have been in disgrace for seven days? Confine her outside the camp for seven days; after that she can be brought back." Then at least I knew my banishment was temporary, my disease would be healed.

Now I see that my enemies were not merely buried in the sea but in my own heart as well. Still, God has let me live, and I believe he will heal me. Though he brings grief, he will yet show compassion. One thing I know, he has hurled my pride into the sea, and for that I will also sing his praises.

Though Scripture doesn't reveal Miriam's thoughts or the attitude of her heart after she was chastened for complaining about Moses, it is not unreasonable to think she would have repented during the seven days of her banishment. After all, it's not easy for a person of faith, however flawed, to hear God speaking as though he were spitting on her and still hold fast to her error.

Perhaps Miriam, and the nation itself, needed a shocking rebuke in order to recognize the seriousness of a sin that threatened the unity of God's people.

Why, you might ask, wasn't Aaron similarly afflicted for his sin? Perhaps because Miriam seemed to be the ringleader. Perhaps, also, because God didn't want the worship at the tabernacle to be disrupted by Aaron's absence as high priest.

The last we hear of Miriam is that she died and was buried in Kadesh-Barnea, not all that far from where Hagar, another slave woman, had encountered an angel in the wilderness so many years earlier. Like her brothers Moses and Aaron, Miriam died shortly before the Israelites ended their forty-year sojourn in the desert. She, too, was prevented from entering the Promised Land.

Still, like them, Miriam is one of the great heroes of our faith. As a young girl, she helped save the infant Moses, Israel's future deliverer. Herself a prophetess, she exhorted and encouraged God's people and led the singing of the first psalm ever recorded in Scripture. Yet, strong though she was, she sinned against God and suffered a punishment designed to bring her to repentance.

Her Legacy of Prayer

Sing to the LORD, for he is highly exalted. The horse and its rider he has hurled into the sea.

—*Exodus 15:21*

REFLECT ON: Numbers 12:1–15.

PRAISE GOD: That he disciplines those he loves, every child who belongs to him.

OFFER THANKS: That God's anger lasts only for a moment but his favor lasts forever.

CONFESS: Any arrogance that may have crept into your
                             heart, especially as it relates to your role at
                             church or at work.

ASK GOD: To help you remember that discipline is an
                             expression of his love for his children.

Lift Your Heart

*I*f a woman like Miriam could act in a way so displeasing to God,
certainly we, too, are capable of sinning, no matter what we have done
for him in the past. Take time this week to do some honest soul-
searching. If you discover anything displeasing to God, ask for his
forgiveness. Don't just whisper a quick prayer and be done with it; let
him know your repentance is sincere. Consider collecting a few small
stones and then driving to the nearest river, lake, or pond. Take a
leisurely walk along the water and tell God again of your sorrow. Then
deliberately hurl each stone into the water, remembering Miriam's song
of praise. Thank God for delivering you from your sins just as he delivered the Israelites from Pharaoh's pursuing army.

Father, thank you for the times you've brought me up short, for loving
me enough to discipline me. Help me be quick to repent, to see my sin
so that you needn't rub my face in it. Then let me experience the joy
that comes from receiving your forgiveness.

12

RAHAB

Her Name Means "Storm,"
"Arrogance," "Broad," or "Spacious"

HER CHARACTER:	Rahab was both clever and wise. She saw judgment coming and was able to devise an escape plan for herself and her family. As soon as she heard what God had done for the Israelites, she cast her lot with his people, risking her life in an act of faith.
HER SORROW:	To see her own people destroyed and her city demolished.
HER JOY:	That God had given her, an idolater and prostitute, the opportunity to know him and belong to his people.
KEY SCRIPTURES:	Joshua 2:1–21; 6:17–25; Matthew 1:5; Hebrews 11:31; James 2:25

ᢞ

*J*ericho may be the world's oldest city. Established nearly six thousand years before Miriam and Moses completed their desert wanderings, its ancient ruins can be found just seventeen miles northeast of Jerusalem. Gateway to Canaan, it was also the home of a prostitute named Rahab, whose house nestled snugly into its thick surrounding walls.

As well as entertaining locals, Rahab welcomed guests from various caravans whose routes crisscrossed Jericho. Men from all over the

East brought news of a swarm of people encamped east of the Jordan. Rahab heard marvelous stories about the exploits of the God of the Israelites. How he had dried up the Red Sea so they could escape their Egyptian slave masters. How he had given them victory in battle against Sihon and Og, two kings of the Amorites. For forty years the God of the Israelites had trained and toughened them in the desert. Such rumors spread fear in Jericho.

While men talked, another man planned. Moses was dead, and he, Joshua, son of Nun, had been appointed leader of the Israelites. Forty years ago Joshua had spied out the land along with Caleb and a group of others, urging the Israelites to take hold of the land of promise. This time there would be no shrinking back. Once the Israelites crossed the Jordan River and destroyed Jericho, the land would open like a melon with the rind peeled back. He could taste the victory.

Joshua sent two spies to Jericho to probe its secrets. The spies soon made their way to Rahab's house, where she hid them beneath stalks of flax drying on the roof. Later that day, Rahab received a message from the king of Jericho, asking her about the spies who had taken refuge in her house.

"Yes, the men came to me, but I did not know where they had come from," she lied to the king's messenger. "At dusk, when it was time to close the city gate, the men left. I don't know which way they went. Go after them quickly. You may catch up with them."

As soon as the king's men left, she hurried to the roof, quickly warning her two guests: "I know that the Lord has given this land to you and that a great fear of you has fallen on us. The Lord your God is God in heaven above and on the earth below. Now then, please swear to me by the Lord that you will show kindness to my family, because I have shown kindness to you. Give me a sure sign that you will spare the lives of my father and mother, my brothers and sisters, and all who belong to them, and that you will save us from death."

To this remarkable statement of faith, the men replied, "Our lives for your lives!" thus sealing the bargain.

Quickly, the two spies handed Rahab a scarlet cord, instructing her to tie it in the window on the side of the house built into the city wall. The invading Israelites would see it and spare everyone inside. Then Rahab instructed the men to hide themselves in the hills for three days until their pursuers abandoned the chase. With that, they slipped out the window and scrambled down the walls of Jericho.

Joshua was smiling long after the spies had left him with their good report. Now was the time to move. He marshaled the people and led them across the Jordan. Though the river was at flood stage, a massive army of Israelites crossed on dry ground. God was with them just as he had been when they left Egypt. Only this time, no one was chasing them—Israel had become the pursuing army, ready for battle!

The news that the waters of the River Jordan had parted for the Israelites terrified the inhabitants of Jericho. Rahab watched anxiously from her window in the wall as the Israelites gathered around the city like a growing storm. Would these fierce warriors with their powerful God remember the scarlet cord? For the thousandth time she reminded her family, especially the little ones, not to take even one step outside the house, lest they perish.

That first day Rahab watched as seven priests carrying an ark led thousands of men around the city. She braced herself, but nothing happened. The next day and the next, for five more days it continued. Then, as the sun was rising on the seventh day, the men of Israel marched again, encircling Jericho seven times. Suddenly, she heard the ram's horn sound and then a thunderous cry, loud enough to split a mountain. The city walls shattered and the Israelites rushed in. Rahab tried to plug her ears to the mayhem outside her home. When the battle of Jericho was over, Rahab and those she loved were spared. Her faith had saved not only herself but her entire household from the terrible judgment decreed for her city.

Jericho's end reminds us of Sodom's. In Sodom, Lot and his daughters were spared; in Jericho, it was Rahab and her family who were spared. But unlike Lot or his wife, Rahab never once hesitated. She is the only woman singled out by name and commended for her faith as part of the great "cloud of witnesses" mentioned in the book of Hebrews. A prostitute living in the midst of an idolatrous people, Rahab was like a brand plucked from the fire. Her own people destroyed, she left everything behind, becoming an ancestor of King David and, therefore, one of Jesus' ancestors as well.

Rahab's story is a dramatic one. It shows us that God's grace accepts no boundaries. The red cord that saved Rahab and her family reminds us of the red blood of Jesus, who still saves us today, and of Isaiah's words, "Though your sins are like scarlet, they shall be as white as snow" (Isaiah 1:18). Rahab put her faith in the God of Israel and was not disappointed.

Her Legacy of Prayer

> "I know that the LORD has given this land to you and that a great fear of you has fallen on us, so that all who live in this country are melting in fear because of you. We have heard how the LORD dried up the water of the Red Sea for you when you came out of Egypt. . . . Now then, please swear to me by the LORD that you will show kindness to my family, because I have shown kindness to you."
> —*Joshua 2:9–10, 12*

REFLECT ON: Joshua 2:1–21.

PRAISE GOD: For giving women key roles in his plan of salvation.

OFFER THANKS: That no one, including ourselves, is beyond the reach of grace.

CONFESS: Our unwillingness to take risks in order to follow God.

ASK GOD: To increase your awe of him.

Lift Your Heart

$\mathcal{U}$se a small red ribbon as a bookmark, tie a red ribbon around the pot of a favorite plant, or place some decorative red roping around a dried floral arrangement to remind you of the vital importance of living by faith. Each time you notice your scarlet cord, let it remind you of the lengths Jesus went to rescue you. Ask him to watch over and protect every member of your family, just as God protected Rahab's family. Say a prayer, asking God to increase your faith, which, after all, is what your life and the vitality of your relationship with God depend on.

Father, I praise you for the wonderful and unexpected ways you have acted in my life. Let the knowledge of your faithfulness increase my courage to take the risks that faith demands.

— 13 —

DEBORAH

Her Name Means "Honey Bee"

HER CHARACTER:	Her vision of the world was shaped not by the political situation of her day but by her relationship with God. Though women in the ancient world did not usually become political leaders, Deborah was just the leader Israel needed—a prophetess who heard God and believed him, whose courage aroused the people, enabling them to throw off foreign oppression.
HER SORROW:	That her people had sunk into despair because of their idolatry, forgetting God's promises and the faith of their ancestors.
HER JOY:	That God turned the enemy's strength on its head, bestowing power to the weak and blessing the land with peace for forty years.
KEY SCRIPTURE:	Judges 4–5

Jericho, gateway to Canaan, had lain in ruins for two hundred years. From there, the Israelites had swept across the country like a storm of locusts, devouring everything in their path. But the native peoples had somehow managed to survive, and like well-rooted weeds, their idolatry spread until it began to strangle Israel's faith.

Rahab and Joshua were the palest of memories now, and the slaves-turned-warriors were once again underdogs, oppressed for twenty years by a coalition of Canaanite rulers, whose chief warrior was Sisera. His nine hundred iron-plated chariots terrified the ill-armed Israelite people, threatening to sweep over them with invincible force. Small wonder no one challenged him.

Sisera must have felt smugly secure, especially since Israel was now led by a woman. But his military calculations failed to account for one key variable: the strategic power of that woman's faith. Deborah was a prophetess who held court under a palm tree several miles northwest of Jericho. Though much of Israel was divided and dispirited, she refused to lose heart. How could she forget God's faithfulness, living so close to ruined Jericho?

She summoned Barak, a Jew from the north, and told him plainly: "The Lord, the God of Israel, commands you: 'Go, take with you ten thousand men of Naphtali and Zebulun and lead the way to Mount Tabor. I will lure Sisera, the commander of Jabin's army, with his chariots and his troops to the Kishon River and give him into your hands.'"

But, like every other man of Israel, Barak was terrified of Sisera, and he refused to comply unless one condition was met: Deborah must accompany him. She would be his talisman on the day of battle. "Very well," she replied, "I will go with you. But because of the way you are going about this, the honor will not be yours, for the Lord will hand Sisera over to a woman."

Hearing of the plot, Sisera led his troops and chariots to the Kishon Wadi, a dry riverbed, determined to crush the uprising. But his very strength turned against him as rain swelled the valley to flood tide. Suddenly, nine hundred iron chariots became a huge liability. No matter how furiously the soldiers flogged their horses, urging them onward, oozing mud held them. They became easy targets for Barak's troops sweeping down from Mount Tabor, putting every man but Sisera to the sword.

Once again, God had heard his people's cries and had sent a deliverer—this time a woman whose faith stilled the voices of doubt and timidity so that the people could hear the one Voice that mattered. On their day of victory, Deborah and Barak sang this song:

> *When the princes in Israel take the lead,*
> > *when the people willingly offer themselves—*
> > *praise the Lord!*
> *Hear this, you kings! Listen, you rulers!*
> > *I will sing to the Lord, I will sing;*
> > *I will make music to the Lord, the God of Israel. . . .*
> *Village life in Israel ceased,*
> > *ceased until I, Deborah, arose,*
> > *arose a mother in Israel.*

Indeed, a mother in Israel had arisen, a woman whose strong faith gave birth to hope and freedom and a peace that lasted forty years. Never again would the Canaanites join forces against Israel. Like an ancient Joan of Arc, Deborah arose and called the people to battle, leading them out of idolatry and restoring their dignity as God's chosen ones.

Her Legacy of Prayer

> *"Hear this, you kings! Listen, you rulers! I will sing to the LORD, I will sing; I will make music to the LORD, the God of Israel."*
>
> —*Judges 5:3*

REFLECT ON: Judges 4.

PRAISE GOD: For speaking clearly to his people.

OFFER THANKS: That God gives prophets to the church, women as well as men.

CONFESS: Anything that makes you reluctant to listen for God's voice.

ASK GOD: To help you discern his voice.

Lift Your Heart

*I*t's difficult, even unpleasant, to listen to two pieces of music at once. Likewise, it's hard to listen to God's voice at the same time you are listening to voices of confusion, discouragement, and condemnation. Deborah's peace and confidence as a leader stemmed in part from her ability to hear God clearly. This week ask the Holy Spirit to help you distinguish God's voice from all the background noise. Ask for grace to discipline your thoughts in order to hear God better. As you pray, put on some quiet background music to remind you to tune in to the one Voice worth listening to.

Lord, I want to hear your voice. Help me to recognize and resist all the phony voices that masquerade as yours. Help me to distinguish yours from all the others. Make me a woman who both listens and speaks your word.

JAEL

Her Name Means
"A Wild or Mountain Goat"

HER CHARACTER:	Decisive and courageous, she seized the opportunity to slay an enemy of God's people.
HER JOY:	To be lauded by Deborah and Barak for her part in a decisive victory.
KEY SCRIPTURE:	Judges 4–5

ael had heard rumors of war. She and her husband, Heber, were Kenites, members of a nomadic tribe whose survival depended on its ability to stay clear of local disputes. Her husband had made his peace with the Canaanites despite his descent from Hobab, Moses' brother-in-law. The ancient ties no longer seemed expedient, however, considering the power of the Canaanite rulers.

Jael watched uneasily through the flaps of her tent as clouds swept the blue from the sky and rain fell like a giant shroud covering the horizon. Sisera, she knew, had marched to Tabor. What good were iron chariots in a flooded valley? she wondered. Yet the Israelites were poorly armed, with little chance of prevailing. Still, she remembered the stories of Moses and the people he had led across the wilderness. Had their God been asleep these many years?

The sight of a man running, then stumbling toward her interrupted her thoughts. A soldier fleeing? Was he Israelite or Canaanite? His identity would, perhaps, reveal the way the winds of battle were blowing.

She went out to meet him, surprised to find that Sisera himself was approaching.

"Come, my lord, come right in. Don't be afraid," she welcomed him.

"I'm thirsty," he said. "Please give me some water." Instead Jael opened a skin of milk, gave him a drink, and covered him.

"Stand in the doorway of the tent," he told her. "If someone comes by and asks you, 'Is anyone here?' say 'No.'"

As soon as Sisera fell into an exhausted asleep, Jael picked up a tent peg and hammer. Her arm was steady, her aim sure. Hadn't she been in charge of the tents all these years? Quickly, she thrust the peg through his temple and into the ground. Like a piece of canvas fixed in place, Sisera, the great general, lay dead, slain by a woman's hand, just as Deborah had prophesied to Barak.

Was Jael a hero, an opportunist, or merely a treacherous woman? It is difficult to know. Perhaps she believed in Israel's God. Perhaps she merely wanted to curry favor with the Israelites, the day's clear winners. Certainly Barak and Deborah approved of her, singing:

Most blessed of women be Jael,
    the wife of Heber the Kenite,
    most blessed of tent-dwelling women.
He asked for water, and she gave him milk;
    in a bowl fit for nobles she brought him curdled milk.
Her hand reached for the tent peg,
    her right hand for the workman's hammer.
She struck Sisera, she crushed his head,
    she shattered and pierced his temple.
At her feet he sank,
    he fell; there he lay.
At her feet he sank, he fell;
    where he sank, there he fell—dead.

Jael's treachery and Deborah's gloating strike us as bloodthirsty, all the more so because we don't usually attribute such behavior to women. But by the standards of ancient warfare, both were heroes. Both were decisive and courageous women who helped God's people at a critical moment in history.

Her Legacy of Prayer

Most blessed of women be Jael. . . . She struck Sisera, she crushed his head, she shattered and pierced his temple. At her feet he sank, he fell; there he lay.

—*Judges 5:24–27*

REFLECT ON: Judges 5.

PRAISE GOD: That he defeats the enemies of our soul.

OFFER THANKS: That we can be instruments of deliverance for others.

CONFESS: Any tendency toward passivity in your struggle against sin and Satan.

ASK GOD: To give you wisdom and discernment in the spiritual battle.

Lift Your Heart

Sometimes we are naive about the kinds of spiritual struggles that face us as Christians. Ephesians 6 talks about the importance of putting on the full armor of God in order to successfully engage in battle. Take some time for a wardrobe check—make sure you aren't missing anything vital, without which you will be more vulnerable to attack. Here's a quick checklist for the well-dressed spiritual warrior:

The Belt of Truth—Have any small dishonesties crept into your life?

The Breastplate of Righteousness—Are you cooperating with grace to become more Christlike?

The Shoes of the Gospel of Peace—The gospel reconciles us to God and others. Are you willing to receive it, live by it, and share it?

The Shield of Faith—Are you responding to life with faith or in a way that shows you really don't think God is quite as loving or as powerful as he says he is?

The Helmet of Salvation—Salvation is a gift. But like any gift, it has to be received.

The Sword of the Spirit—God's Word wounds the enemy and thwarts his purposes. Reading and praying through Scripture helps us take the offensive.

Lord, help me to be ready so that any moment I am equipped to stand against the enemy and even deal a decisive blow in the battle. Give me courage, discernment, and wisdom, and help me to stay close to you in the midst of the fray.

$$\text{———} \quad 15 \quad \text{———}$$

DELILAH

Her Name Means "Dainty One"

HER CHARACTER:	A harlot whose nationality is unknown, she used her beauty to betray her lover and enrich herself.
HER SORROW:	That Samson lied to her, making her look foolish on three different occasions.
HER JOY:	That she overpowered one of history's most powerful men, handing him over to his enemy, the Philistines.
KEY SCRIPTURE:	Judges 16:4–22

Her teeth gleamed white in the dusky light as a smile parted lips soft and smooth as a scarlet ribbon. Earrings glinted gold as she threw back her head and laughed out loud. Fortune had come knocking on her door that day. No lover had ever paid Delilah so well as Samson would.

The Philistine kings hated the long-haired strongman who had set their fields afire and slain a thousand of their countrymen. Each had offered an incredible sum—eleven hundred shekels of silver! She had merely to deliver the secret of Samson's strength. His would be no match for hers, a strength born of beauty and schooled in the arts of love. Weakened by passion, he would tell her everything she needed to know.

"If anyone ties me with seven fresh thongs that have not been dried, I'll become as any other man," he replied to her persistent probing. Hiding a few Philistines in the room for good measure, she waited until he slept and then carefully wrapped him with the thongs and exclaimed, "Samson, the Philistines are upon you!" But he had outsmarted her, snapping the cords as his enemies fled.

Like a man toying with a kitten, Samson repeated the ruse twice, tricking Delilah with crazy stories about new ropes and braided hair. Finally Delilah confronted him, "How can you say, 'I love you,' when you won't confide in me? This is the third time you have made a fool of me and haven't told me the secret of your great strength." Worn down by her nagging, Samson gave in.

"No razor has ever been used on my head," he confided, "because I have been a Nazirite set apart to God since birth. If my head were shaved, my strength would leave me, and I would become as weak as any other man." Years earlier, before his birth, an angel had instructed his mother that he should drink no wine, touch nothing unclean, and never cut his hair. He was to be dedicated to God in a special way, destined to play a great role in God's plan to free his people from their Philistine overlords. A strong man unable to subdue his own tempestuous nature, Samson had already broken the first two stipulations of his vow. Now he broke the third, preferring the good graces of a woman to the favor of his God.

Sensing she had heard the truth at last, Delilah sent word to the Philistines. After cutting his hair while he slept, she once again called, "Samson, the Philistines are upon you!" This time Samson awoke from his sleep unable to resist his enemies, who quickly seized him, gouging out his eyes. Then they imprisoned him in Gaza, where he spent his days in darkness, performing women's work grinding grain.

That's the last we hear of the lovely, treacherous, and now wealthy Delilah, but not the last we hear of her lover. Slowly Samson's hair began to grow back, first a short cap to warm his head and then a cover for his ears. What harm could a blind man do them? the Philistines must have reasoned.

One day the Philistines held a great celebration in honor of Dagon, god of the harvest, for delivering Samson into their hands. Oblivious to their danger, they brought him out of prison to make sport of their once-mighty enemy. But when Samson stood among the pillars of their temple, he prayed, "O Sovereign Lord, remember me. O God, please strengthen me just once more, and let me with one blow get revenge on the Philistines for my two eyes." Then he braced himself against the two central pillars of the temple and pushed. The roof buckled and collapsed, and Samson and his enemies were buried together under its rubble. By his death, Samson killed more Philistines than he had in life. Just as the angel had predicted, Samson had begun a work of deliverance that David would complete many years later.

The strange story of Samson and Delilah is hardly edifying. It's tempting to conclude that the selfish, ill-disciplined Samson had finally met his match in the greedy Delilah. A visitation by an angel, the gift of supernatural strength, a prophetic destiny—such obvious blessings could not assure Samson's devotion. Why would God use such a man, enabling him to become a judge in Israel? What a contrast to Deborah, who had ruled Israel a century earlier! Perhaps God had little promising material to choose from, given the state of his people during an era of Israel's history where "everyone did as he saw fit" (Judges 21:25).

If anything, Delilah's role in this sordid tale assures us that God will use anything and anyone to accomplish his purpose. Even our sin. Even our enemies. Our deliverance is purely a matter of grace. But how much better if we become people set apart for his service, whose inner strengths match our outer strengths, enabling us to live out our destiny assured of God's pleasure.

Her Legacy of Prayer

"How can you say, 'I love you,' when you won't confide in me? This is the third time you have made a fool of me and haven't told me the secret of your great strength." With such nagging she prodded him day after day until he was tired to death.

—Judges 16:15–16

REFLECT ON:	Judges 16:4–22.
PRAISE GOD:	That he is sovereign, able to use our most tangled relationships to achieve his purposes.
OFFER THANKS:	For calling you to be devoted to him, set apart in a special way.
CONFESS:	Any tendency to manipulate others.
ASK GOD:	To help you surrender any unhealthy relationship to him. Take whatever steps God is calling you to take.

Lift Your Heart

Take inventory of your most important relationships. Have you formed any unhealthy dependencies? Is a spouse or boyfriend leading you away from God rather than closer to him? Have you made compromises that diminish your desire for God? If so, find a trusted friend or counselor in which to confide. Pray together about the best course of action and then follow it. Be faithful to marital commitments, but find a way to restore your spiritual passion. Right now, take time to write God a letter. Tell him how desirable he is and how much you long to be connected to him. Don't be afraid to wear your heart on your sleeve—God is looking for men and women who love him more than they love their own lives.

_____

Lord, you know all the struggles of my heart. You created me in such a way that no one but you can fully satisfy my longings. Yet you also know how easily I am fooled, believing that flesh and blood relationships hold the key to all my needs. Forgive me for the times I've put my relationship with _____ above my relationship with you. Give me the wisdom, courage, and grace to love you with abandon.

— 16 —

NAOMI

Her Name Means
"My Joy" or "Pleasant"

HER CHARACTER:	Suffering a threefold tragedy, Naomi refused to hide her sorrow or bitterness. Believing in God's sovereignty, she attributed her suffering to his will. But her fixation on circumstances, both past and present, led to hopelessness. A kind and loving mother-in-law, she inspired unusual love and loyalty in her daughters-in-law.
HER SORROW:	To have lost a husband and two sons in a foreign land, far from family and friends.
HER JOY:	To have returned safely to Bethlehem with her daughter-in-law Ruth, who would eventually rekindle her happiness and hope.
KEY SCRIPTURE:	Ruth 1; 4:13–17

꙳

She stood like an old tree twisted against the sky. The wind that swept the hillside blew through her as though her body were hollow. Naomi could not remember what it felt like to be full, to feel secure. Though she could see for miles from her vantage point high on the road that led from Moab to Judah, she could glimpse nothing at all of her future. She thought about robbers, rumored on the road ahead. What more, she wondered, could possibly be taken from her? Her thoughts strayed to the past.

Moses, she knew, had been buried somewhere in these mountains. But his people and hers had moved west into Canaan centuries earlier. Would she, too, be left behind, prevented from ever seeing her kinsfolk again? Was God so displeased with her?

Ten years ago, she and Elimelech had lived happily in Bethlehem. But the city whose name meant "house of bread" suddenly had none, so they had migrated to the highlands of Moab to escape the famine. Then Elimelech had died and her sons had married Moabite women, whose race had descended from Abraham's nephew, Lot. Plenty of women lost their husbands. Like them, she would find a way to survive. But then she had suffered the worst grief a mother could— outliving her own children.

Now Ruth and Orpah, her daughters-in-law, were the only kin she had in Moab. Loving them tenderly, she felt their widowhood as a double grief. Together they had cried and comforted each other, finally deciding to leave Moab for Bethlehem. But once on the road, Naomi's misgivings outran her craving for companionship. It wasn't right for young women to forsake their families and friends for so uncertain a future. What chance would they, widows and strangers, have in Bethlehem, even now that the famine had run its course?

"Go back, each of you, to your mother's home," she told them. "May the Lord show kindness to you, as you have shown to your dead and to me. May the Lord grant that each of you will find rest in the home of another husband."

But Orpah and Ruth insisted, "We will go back with you to your people."

"Why would you come with me? Am I going to have any more sons, who could become your husbands? Return home, my daughters; I am too old to have another husband. Even if I thought there was still hope for me—even if I had a husband tonight and then gave birth to sons—would you wait until they grew up?"

The three women embraced, tears streaking their cheeks. Then Orpah kissed her mother-in-law good-bye. But Ruth clutched Naomi and whispered fiercely, "Where you go I will go, and where you stay I will stay. Your people will be my people and your God my God. Where you die I will die, and there I will be buried. May the Lord deal with me, be it ever so severely, if anything but death separates you and me."

The old woman's stubbornness was no match for the younger woman's love. And so Naomi and Ruth continued on to Bethlehem. After so long an absence, Naomi's return created a great commotion in the town, and all the women welcomed her, saying, "Can this be Naomi?"

"Don't call me Naomi," she told them. "Call me Mara [meaning 'bitter'], because the Almighty has made my life very bitter. I went away full, but the Lord has brought me back empty. The Lord has afflicted me; the Almighty has brought misfortune upon me."

Naomi could not see past her suffering. Like many of us, she may have felt her tragedies were punishment for her sins. Yet had she known the blessings still in store, she might not have felt so hopeless. Instead, she might have compared herself to the tree that the book of Job so graciously describes:

> There is hope for a tree: If it is cut down, it will sprout again, and its new shoots will not fail. Its roots may grow old in the ground and its stump die in the soil, yet at the scent of water it will bud and put forth shoots like a plant. (Job 14:7–9)

Though she didn't know it, the scent of water was in the air. Naomi's life was beginning again, her story still unfolding.

Her Legacy of Prayer

> *"Where you go I will go, and where you stay I will stay. Your people will be my people and your God my God. Where you die I will die, and there I will be buried. May the LORD deal with me, be it ever so severely, if anything but death separates you and me."*
>
> —Ruth 1:16–17

REFLECT ON:	Ruth 1.
PRAISE GOD:	For creating us with the power to form deep and lasting relationships.
OFFER THANKS:	For the variety of friends God has given you.
CONFESS:	Your tendency to be too busy to pay attention to your friends or too preoccupied with your own concerns to take time for theirs.
ASK GOD:	To make you a more loyal and loving friend in the year ahead.

Lift Your Heart

Think about someone with whom you used to be especially close. Perhaps time or distance has eroded the friendship. Wax nostalgic as you recall the great meals, oddball jokes, late-night conversations, or crazy adventures you shared. Wouldn't it be great to have that person back in your life? Pick up the phone or write a letter to renew the friendship. If the other person seems willing, invest some energy rebuilding the relationship in the year ahead. Let your memories form a foundation for your friendship, but don't stop there—get busy making new ones. If she's nearby, have her over for a meal or a fancy dessert. If not, exchange family photos. Stay in touch by email. If you can afford to, you can even meet halfway for a weekend excursion.

Lord, thank you for the blessing of friends who, by sharing their lives with us, double our joys and halve our sorrows. Help me to cherish the friends you've given me and to become the kind of friend others will cherish: a woman who listens, encourages, and keeps confidences; a woman who knows how to laugh and how to cry; a woman who is loyal, forgiving, and loving.

17

RUTH

Her Name Means
"Friendship"

HER CHARACTER:	Generous, loyal, and loving, she is strong and serene, able to take unusual risks, dealing actively with the consequences.
HER SORROW:	To have lost her husband, homeland, and family.
HER JOY:	To discover firsthand the generous, loyal, and loving nature of God, as he provided her with a husband, a son, and a home to call her own.
KEY SCRIPTURES:	Ruth 2–4; Matthew 1:5

*I*t was harvest time in Israel when Boaz first laid eyes on the young woman. The sun painted the fields a tawny gold as workers swung their sickles in even rhythms through the standing grain. According to Israel's law and custom, the poor had the right to gather whatever the harvesters missed.

Ruth toiled quickly and efficiently, he noticed, stuffing grain into a coarse sack slung across her shoulder. Strands of black hair escaped her head covering, softly framing olive-colored skin, still smooth despite the sun. She rested, but only for a moment, her eyes wary for any sign of trouble from the men working the fields. Gleaning was rough work and dangerous, especially for an attractive young foreigner, alone and unprotected.

Everyone in Bethlehem had been talking about Boaz's relative, Naomi, and her unexpected return. Ruth, he knew, had come with her. He had heard of their shared tragedy and the extraordinary loyalty the younger had displayed toward the older mother-in-law, even promising to renounce Moab's idols for Israel's God. A man could wish for such a friend as Ruth had been to Naomi.

Determined to repay her kindness in some way, Boaz called to her, "My daughter, listen to me. Don't go and glean in another field and don't go away from here. Stay here with my servant girls. Watch the field where the men are harvesting, and follow along after the girls. I have told the men not to touch you." The young woman smiled her agreement.

Later he spoke to Ruth again, this time offering bread and roasted grain for her dinner. When she finished eating, he instructed his men to pull out some stalks of grain and strew them in her path. It was good to see her leaving that night with a bulging harvest sack.

Day after day, he watched her, aware that the wheat and barley harvest were too soon drawing to a close. One evening, he and the other men were winnowing barley on the threshing floor. After he had finished eating and drinking, he lay down under the stars at the far end of the grain pile. With so many men to guard the harvest, robbers wouldn't dare approach. But in the middle of the night he woke with a start, realizing that someone had dared. To his surprise, he discovered the intruder was neither a robber nor a man, but a woman who lay at his feet.

She, too, was awake. "I am your servant, Ruth," she whispered. "Spread the corner of your garment over me, since you are a kinsman-redeemer."

He could hardly believe her words. The young woman had taken a remarkable risk, appearing at night and lying down so close to him. Quickly, he covered her, saying, "The Lord bless you. This kindness is greater than that which you showed earlier: You have not run after the younger men, whether rich or poor. And now, my daughter, don't be afraid. I will do for you all you ask." So Ruth lay at his feet until morning, rising before the early light could reveal her presence to others.

But Boaz knew of an obstacle that could yet spoil things. Naomi had a closer relative than he, a man who could play the role of kinsman-redeemer, marrying Ruth and restoring her dead husband's name. This man was entitled to purchase a field belonging to Naomi, but according to the law, to purchase the field he had to marry Ruth as well. One word from him could destroy Boaz's hope of making Ruth his wife.

Boaz wasted no time putting the case before the man, who seemed interested enough in the land. But as soon as the man discovered that marriage was part of the bargain, he relinquished his rights to the land to Boaz.

So the two were married and the older man welcomed the young woman into his home. And God blessed them with a son, whom they named Obed.

Pulling Ruth close to him, Boaz watched one day as Naomi held her grandson to her breast. Surrounded by the other women of Bethlehem, she looked young again, more like the woman he remembered when her husband, Elimelech, had been alive. He watched as the women talked with Ruth regarding the child: "Praise be to the Lord, who this day has not left you without a kinsman-redeemer. May he become famous throughout Israel! He will renew your life and sustain you in your old age. For your daughter-in-law, who loves you and who is better to you than seven sons, has given him birth."

Yes, Boaz thought, his Ruth was better to Naomi than seven sons. And he was grateful for the friendship between the two women. Had Ruth and Naomi gone their separate ways, his life would have been so much the poorer.

The good-hearted Boaz felt strong and young again. But even he couldn't have realized how greatly God had blessed him in the person of Ruth. For their son Obed became the father of Jesse, and Jesse the father of David. In addition to being King David's great-grandparents, both Boaz and Ruth are mentioned in the genealogy of Jesus of

Nazareth, who is, after all, our own great Kinsman-Redeemer, uniting us to himself, healing our sorrows, and giving us, as well, a future full of hope.

Her Legacy of Prayer

The women said to Naomi, "Praise be to the LORD, who this day has not left you without a kinsman-redeemer. May he become famous throughout Israel! He will renew your life and sustain you in your old age. For your daughter-in-law, who loves you and who is better to you than seven sons, has given him birth."

—*Ruth 4:14–15*

REFLECT ON: Ruth 3–4.

PRAISE GOD: That he provides for those who have no one to provide for them.

OFFER THANKS: For the way God has used other women, your mother or mother-in-law, your sisters or daughters, to provide for you.

CONFESS.   Any tendency to compete with other women.

ASK GOD: To help you appreciate your own mother and mother-in-law and to give you a vision for the power of two women, linked by love and faith.

Lift Your Heart

*I*t's easy to assume the important women in our lives know how much we cherish them. But Mother's Day cards and friendship cards, nice as they are to get and give, don't really do the trick. We also need to verbalize our love sincerely and regularly. Don't wait until Mother's Day to treat your mother, mother-in-law, or an older friend to tea or a leisurely lunch. Tell her just how much you care about her. (Make sure you take time beforehand to think about all her wonderful qualities. Take notes so that you can be specific.) You might even buy a small blank book and record all the ways she's blessed you. Decorate each page with colorful stickers or stencils. Package it with scented soap and bath salts and give it as a keepsake she can treasure.

———————————————

Father, I thank you for the women who have played such an important role in my life. Please bless each one in a special way today and help me find ways to express to them my love and gratitude.

18

HANNAH

Her Name Means
"Graciousness" or "Favor"

HER CHARACTER: Provoked by another woman's malice, she refused to respond in kind. Instead, she poured out her hurt and sorrow to God, allowing him to vindicate her.

HER SORROW: To be taunted and misunderstood.

HER JOY: To proclaim God's power and goodness, his habit of raising the lowly and humbling the proud.

KEY SCRIPTURES: 1 Samuel 1:1–2:11; 2:19–21

It was only fifteen miles, but every year the journey from Ramah to Shiloh, to worship at the tabernacle, seemed longer. At home, Hannah found ways to avoid her husband's second wife, but once in Shiloh there was no escaping her taunts. Hannah felt like a leaky tent in a driving rain, unable to defend herself against the harsh weather of the other woman's heart.

Even Elkanah's arm around her provided no shelter. "Hannah, why are you weeping? Why don't you eat? Why are you downhearted? Don't I mean more to you than ten sons?" *Yes, she has given me children, but it's you I love. Ignore her taunts.*

How could Hannah make him understand that even the best of men could not erase a woman's longing for children? His attempt at comforting her only sharpened the pain, heightening her sense of isolation.

Hannah stood for a long time at the tabernacle, weeping and praying. Her lips moved without making a sound as her heart poured out its grief to God: "O Lord Almighty, if you will only look upon your servant's misery and remember me, and not forget your servant but give her a son, then I will give him to the Lord for all the days of his life, and no razor will ever be used on his head."

The priest Eli was used to people coming to Shiloh to celebrate the feasts, eating and drinking more than they should. Watching Hannah from his chair by the doorpost of the temple, he wondered why her shoulders were shaking, her lips moving without making a sound. She must be drunk, he concluded. So he interrupted her silent prayer with a rebuke: "How long will you keep on getting drunk? Get rid of your wine."

"Not so, my lord," Hannah defended herself. "I am a woman who is deeply troubled. I have not been drinking wine or beer; I was pouring out my soul to the Lord. Do not take your servant for a wicked woman; I have been praying here out of my great anguish and grief."

Satisfied by her explanation, Eli blessed her, saying, "May the God of Israel grant you what you have asked of him."

Early the next morning, Hannah and Elkanah returned to their home in Ramah, where Hannah at last conceived. Soon she held against her shoulder the tiny child she had yearned for, the child she had dedicated to God. After Samuel was weaned, she would take him to Eli at Shiloh. Like Jochebed placing the child Moses into the waters of the Nile as though into God's own hands, she would surrender her child to the priest's care. Eventually Hannah's boy would become a prophet and Israel's last judge. His hands would anoint both Saul and David as Israel's first kings.

Like Sarah and Rachel, Hannah grieved over the children she couldn't have. But unlike them, she took her anguish directly to God. Misunderstood by both her husband and her priest, she could easily have turned her sorrow on herself or others, becoming bitter, hopeless, or vindictive. But instead of merely pitying herself or responding in kind, she poured out her soul to God. And God graciously answered her prayer.

Each year Hannah presented Samuel with a little robe she had sewn. And each year, the priest Eli blessed her husband, Elkanah, saying, "May the Lord give you children by this woman to take the place of the one she prayed for and gave to the Lord." And so Hannah became the mother of three more sons and two daughters. Her great prayer, echoed nearly a thousand years later by Mary's Magnificat, expresses her praise: "My heart rejoices in the Lord; in the Lord my horn is lifted high. My mouth boasts over my enemies, for I delight in your deliverance. . . . The Lord sends poverty and wealth; he humbles and he exalts. He raises the poor from the dust and lifts the needy from the ash heap."

Her Legacy of Prayer

In bitterness of soul Hannah wept much and prayed to the LORD. And she made a vow, saying, "O LORD Almighty, if you will only look upon your servant's misery and remember me, and not forget your servant but give her a son, then I will give him to the LORD for all the days of his life."

— *1 Samuel 1:10–11*

REFLECT ON:	1 Samuel 2:1–10.
PRAISE GOD:	That he knows our hearts.
OFFER THANKS:	For already answering so many of your prayers.
CONFESS:	Your tendency to pour out your heart to everyone but God, making him a last, rather than first, resort.
ASK GOD:	To give you the grace to trust his strength.

Lift Your Heart

*O*ne way to build your confidence in God is to form a habit of remembrance. It's so easy to forget everything he's already done by being preoccupied with what you want him to do right here, right now. But by forgetting his blessings, you form a habit of ingratitude. By frequently thanking God for what he's done, you build a habit of gratitude, which will also deepen your trust in God's compassion, mercy, faithfulness, and power. Find a blank notebook or a lovely scrapbook that can become your Remembrance Book. In it, write down ways in which God has answered your prayers. Keep letters, photos of loved ones, or newspaper clippings—anything that reminds you of answered prayers. Let your Remembrance Book be a tangible way to keep God's faithfulness in the forefront of your heart.

Father, thank you for all the prayers you've answered during my lifetime. You've answered small prayers and big prayers, evening prayers and morning prayers, soft prayers and loud prayers, anxious prayers and peaceful prayers. May my own prayers be shaped according to your faithfulness, becoming less selfish and frantic and more calm and trusting with each day that passes.

19

MICHAL

Her Name Means
"Who Is Like God?"

HER CHARACTER:	A woman of strong emotions, she was unable to control the important circumstances of her life. Forcibly separated from two husbands, she lost her father and her brother, who were savaged by their enemies.
HER SORROW:	That she was ensnared in the drawn-out battle between Saul and David.
HER JOY:	She enjoyed a passionate, albeit short-lived, love for David.
KEY SCRIPTURES:	1 Samuel 18:20–29; 19:11–17; 2 Samuel 6:16–23

Scene One

*M*ichal stretched herself across the window's edge. Leaning out as far as she dared, she could see a man running through the night shadows, his movements swift and graceful, like a young stag evading its predators. Even if her father the king pursued with an army, she was confident he would not catch her David.

She had loved the shepherd boy since the day he had calmed Saul's troubled soul with his harp playing. After he defeated the hideous

Goliath with only a sling and a stone, all Israel fell in love with him. But it was for her alone that David had slain two hundred Philistines—to prove his worth. He made a fit husband for a princess.

She turned from the window, grateful for the chance to have aided her husband's escape. Quickly she dressed one of the household idols, placing it in their bed and topping it with goat's hair to make it look like a sleeping David. She was ready for her father's men when they came pounding on her door.

"He is ill," she told them.

So they returned to King Saul, who immediately ordered them back, saying, "Bring him up to me in his bed so that I may kill him."

Discovering the ruse, Saul confronted his daughter: "Why did you deceive me like this and send my enemy away so that he escaped?"

Michal lowered her eyes and replied, "He said to me, 'Let me get away. Why should I kill you?'" She held her breath, certain her father would never swallow so bold a lie.

Scene Two
(Nine Years Later)

*M*ichal glanced out the window, arms folded tightly against her breast, observing the scene below. David, now the king, had entered Jerusalem, leaping and dancing as the ark of the covenant was carried into Jerusalem. He looked ridiculous, she thought, more like a romping goat than a great king.

David offered the sacrifices and blessed the people. Then he entered his own house to bless it. But Saul's daughter met him with scornful eyes. "How the king of Israel has distinguished himself today, disrobing in the sight of the slave girls of his servants as any vulgar fellow would!"

"It was before the Lord, who chose me," he replied, "rather than your father or anyone from his house when he appointed me ruler over the Lord's people Israel—I will celebrate before the Lord. I will become even more undignified than this, and I will be humiliated in my own eyes. But by these slave girls you spoke of, I will be held in honor."

From then on, silence spread like a shield of ice between them. The queen ended her days alone, with neither children nor family to warm her.

Twice, Michal stood at a window observing David. In the first scene, Scripture paints her as David's wife, in the second as Saul's daughter. In fact, her attitude is so changed that we feel perplexed, watching her as she watches David. To understand what may have shaped Michal's heart in the intervening years, we need to find a corridor connecting the two windows, a passageway that somehow led from love to scorn.

Michal may have expected her separation from David to be a short one, her idealism forging a happy ending to their fairy-tale love. Perhaps she believed David would find a way to protect her from her father's wrath. Was she shocked when real life intervened and her father punished her by marrying her to another man? Did her bitterness grow during David's long absence? Had she finally made peace with her new husband only to be torn from him when David demanded her back after Saul's death? Did she question God's judgments, identifying more with the dead than the living after her father perished in a desperate battle with the Philistines?

Perhaps Michal's bitterness swelled to rage when she realized she had always been someone else's pawn, a mere woman manipulated by powerful men. Her own father used her, promising her to David in hopes she would prove a snare to him. And, finally, one of her brothers handed her back to David after Saul's death, further legitimizing David's claim to the throne. A princess, then a queen, she was still a slave.

Michal's story is tragic. Throughout the difficult circumstances of her life, we see little evidence of a faith to sustain her. Instead, she is tossed back and forth, her heart left to draw its own bitter conclusions. In the last scene with David, we see a woman blind with scorn, making the very mistake God cautioned the prophet Samuel against in his search for a king to succeed the wayward Saul: "Do not consider his appearance or his height. The Lord does not look at the things man looks at. Man looks at the outward appearance, but the Lord looks at the heart" (1 Samuel 16:7).

The truth is, God is the only one who can see into the depths of anyone's heart, including Michal's. He knew everything that had happened, both good and bad. The story of Michal seems to indicate that she grew to be more like Saul than David. As such, she reminds us that even victims have choices. No matter how much we've been sinned against, we still have the power to choose the attitude of our heart. If we cast ourselves on God's mercy, asking him to help us, he cannot refuse. Even in difficulty, he will dwell in us, shaping our own wayward hearts into the likeness of his own.

Her Legacy of Prayer

Now Saul's daughter Michal was in love with David, and when they told Saul about it, he was pleased. "I will give her to him," he thought, "so that she may be a snare to him and so that the hand of the Philistines may be against him."

—1 Samuel 18:20–21

As the ark of the LORD was entering the City of David, Michal daughter of Saul watched from a window. And when she saw King David leaping and dancing before the LORD, she despised him in her heart.

—2 Samuel 6:16

REFLECT ON: 1 Samuel 19:11–17; 2 Samuel 6:16–23.

PRAISE GOD: Because he is the same—yesterday, today, and forever.

OFFER THANKS: That God gives us the freedom to choose how we will respond to him.

CONFESS: Allowing skepticism or cynicism to infiltrate
                            your faith.

ASK GOD: To increase your awe of him.

Lift Your Heart

David was so exuberant that he danced in public as a way of worshiping God. You may not be quite ready to take your joy to the streets, but you can loosen up a bit by raising your hands in prayer, visiting a church whose worship style is a little outside your comfort zone, or just dancing and singing along with a praise and worship tape when no one else is home. Go ahead. Enjoy yourself in God's presence! If he's not worth getting excited about, who is?

Shout with joy to God, all the earth! Sing the glory of his name; make his praise glorious! Say to God, "How awesome are your deeds! So great is your power that your enemies cringe before you. All the earth bows down to you; they sing praise to you, they sing praise to your name" (Psalm 66:1–4).

20

ABIGAIL

Her Name Means
"My Father Is Joy"

HER CHARACTER:	Generous, quick-witted, and wise, she is one of the Bible's great peacemakers.
HER SORROW:	To have been mismatched in marriage to her first husband.
HER JOY:	That God used her to save lives, eventually making her the wife of David.
KEY SCRIPTURE:	1 Samuel 25:2–42

$\mathcal{B}$ lockhead, numskull, nincompoop—the words strike us both harshly and humorously. But any woman married to a man worthy of such labels would have little to laugh about.

Abigail must have felt suffocated, having been paired with just such a husband. Her father may have thought the wealthy Nabal a catch, little realizing the man's domineering attitude might one day endanger his daughter's well-being. But fools and ruin often keep close company, as Abigail soon discovered.

For some time Abigail had been hearing of David: his encounter with Goliath, his ruddy good looks, his prowess in battle, his rift with King Saul. Recently, he had become her near neighbor in the Desert of Maon, west of the Dead Sea, where he had taken refuge from Saul. Since David had arrived with his six hundred men, marauders kept clear of her husband's livestock, and Nabal's flocks prospered as a result.

But when David sent ten of his men to ask Nabal for provisions, Nabal, who had grown richer by the day thanks to David, nearly spit in their faces. "Who is this David? Many servants are breaking away from their masters these days. Why should I take my bread and water, and the meat I have slaughtered for my shearers, and give it to men coming from who knows where?" Rich though he was, Nabal had just foolishly insulted the region's most powerful man.

Aware of their danger, one of the servants ran quickly to Abigail, begging her to intervene. As Nabal's wife, she must have suffered his arrogance every day of her life. But this time his folly jeopardized the entire household. Wasting no time, and without a word to her husband, she loaded a caravan of donkeys with gifts for David and his men—freshly baked bread, skins of wine, red meat, and various delicacies and took them to David's camp. As soon as she saw him, she fell to the ground at his feet, making one of the longest speeches by a woman recorded in the Bible:

"My lord," she pleaded, "let the blame be on me alone. May my lord pay no attention to that wicked man Nabal. He is just like his name—his name is Fool, and folly goes with him. But as for me, your servant, I did not see the men my master sent. Please forgive your servant's offense, for the Lord will certainly make a lasting dynasty for my master, because he fights the Lord's battles. Let no wrongdoing be found in you as long as you live. Even though someone is pursuing you to take your life, the life of my master will be bound securely in the bundle of the living by the Lord your God. But the lives of your enemies he will hurl away as from the pocket of a sling."

These last words, of course, reminded David of his success against Goliath, erasing his anger and enabling his gracious reply: "Praise be to the Lord, the God of Israel, who has sent you today to meet me. May you be blessed for your good judgment and for keeping me from bloodshed this day and from avenging myself with my own hands. If you had not come quickly to meet me, not one male belonging to Nabal would have been left alive by daybreak." In addition to saving lives, Abigail's wisdom had spared David from sinning, reminding him that vengeance belongs only to God.

After her encounter with David, Abigail went to Carmel, where Nabal had been shearing his sheep and celebrating his good fortune. Once again, she found him playing the fool. Oblivious to danger, he was drunkenly presiding over a festival banquet, like a great king. She waited until morning, when he was sober, to tell him what had happened. As soon as Nabal heard the news, his heart failed. Ten days later he was dead.

Arrogance, greed, and selfishness had conspired to rob Nabal of any good sense he might once have possessed. Thinking himself a great man when he was only a small one, he lost everything. Abigail was Nabal's opposite, a woman whose humility, faith, generosity, intelligence, and honesty made her wise. Rather than putting others at risk by an ungoverned tongue, her gracious words saved lives. Few husbands and wives were ever so ill-suited to each other.

When David heard the news of Nabal's death, he sent word to Abigail, asking her to be his wife. This time it was Abigail's choice whether or not to marry. She accepted, becoming David's third wife and eventually mother to his second son, Kileab.

Unlike Michal, who had been a mere pawn on a chessboard, Abigail was a woman who rose above her circumstances to change the course of events. Though Scripture doesn't offer details regarding her daily life, it is logical to suppose she was a good wife to Nabal. Even her entreaty to David was the act of a good wife. Perhaps her virtues were not inborn, but developed in the midst of a difficult marriage. Or perhaps her marriage was actually the catalyst for her character, helping her to cultivate contrasting virtues to Nabal's vices. Regardless, through her quick-witted action, she spared her husband's life and goods. It was God, not Abigail or David, who paid Nabal back for his arrogance and greed.

Her Legacy of Prayer

> *David said to Abigail, "Praise be to the LORD, the God of Israel, who has sent you today to meet me. May you be blessed for your good judgment and for keeping me from bloodshed this day and from avenging myself with my own hands."*
>
> *—1 Samuel 25:32–33*

REFLECT ON: 1 Samuel 25:2–42.

PRAISE GOD: For calling you to be a peacemaker in your family, neighborhood, and world.

OFFER THANKS: That God knows every challenge facing your marriage.

CONFESS: Any bitterness you may have harbored about your marriage.

ASK GOD: To use your relationship with your husband to strengthen your character and increase your faith.

Lift Your Heart

*I*f you haven't yet made a commitment to pray daily for your husband, do so today. Set aside a few minutes to surrender your marriage to God, specifically asking him to bless your spouse. Try to refrain from focusing on your laundry list of complaints and instead pray for the needs you know your husband has. Ask God to shape your marriage relationship and use it for his purposes. Relinquish any desire you may have to control your husband; instead, ask God to work in his life. For help in forming the habit, read *The Power of a Praying Wife* by Stormie Omartian or *When He Doesn't Believe* by Nancy Kennedy.

Father, I ask you to bless my husband in every facet of his life—his health, his work, his relationship with our children, our relationship together, and his relationship to you. Let nothing and no one, including myself, hinder your work in his life.

21

THE WOMAN
OF ENDOR

HER CHARACTER:	Compassionate to Saul on the eve of his death, she exercised power by acting as a medium.
HER SORROW:	To have delivered a hopeless message to Israel's king.
KEY SCRIPTURE:	1 Samuel 28:3–25

It was a night for frightening apparitions. Squinting through the open doorway, the woman stiffened, retreating a step. A face loomed before her, floating on its own like a pale moon in the outer darkness. Before she could close the door, she felt fingers gripping her wrist.

"Please," the voice insisted, "consult a spirit for me, and bring up for me the one I name."

A large man pushed through the door, followed by two more men. She could feel fear enter as he swept past her and sat down on the couch.

"Surely you know what Saul has done. He has cut off the mediums and spiritists from the land. Why have you set a trap for my life to bring about my death?" she replied.

"As surely as the Lord lives, you will not be punished for this," he swore.

"Whom shall I bring up for you?"

"Bring up Samuel," he said.

So the woman sat down and yielded herself, making her soul a bridge for the dead to walk across.

Suddenly she screamed, "Why have you deceived me? You are Saul!"

The king calmed her, saying, "Don't be afraid. What do you see?"

"An old man wearing a robe is coming up," she said.

Saul bowed down and prostrated himself, his face in the dirt.

Samuel said to Saul, "Why have you disturbed me by bringing me up?"

"I am in great distress," Saul replied. "The Philistines are fighting against me, and God has turned away from me. He no longer answers me, either by prophets or by dreams. So I have called on you to tell me what to do."

Samuel said, "Why do you consult me, now that the Lord has turned away from you and become your enemy? The Lord has done what he predicted through me. The Lord has torn the kingdom out of your hands and given it to one of your neighbors—to David. Tomorrow you and your sons will be with me. The Lord will also hand over the army of Israel to the Philistines."

The woman shuddered, the message delivered. Little wonder the king had seemed so desolate. Fear had crushed the life out of his once-strong face, hollowing the eyes, etching deep lines across cheeks and forehead.

Taking pity, she spoke to him: "Look, your maidservant has obeyed you. I took my life in my hands and did what you told me to do. Now please listen to your servant and let me give you some food so you may eat and have the strength to go on your way."

Kindly, she served what was probably Saul's last meal. The next day he was dead. Wounded in battle, he fell on his own sword, determined to finish the job before his enemies could reach him. True to form, Saul, who had always tried to control his destiny, controlled even the manner of his death. But he could not control what happened next. Discovering his body, the Philistines celebrated by severing his head and hanging it in the temple of their god. Then they tacked his naked corpse to the walls of a nearby town as a trophy. Israel's first king had become a gruesome spectacle.

The woman of Endor is a strange character, steeped in the occult yet kind and motherly in her attitude toward the tormented king. For some reason, God allowed her to call up the prophet Samuel even though necromancy (conjuring spirits for the purpose of knowing or influencing future events) was strictly forbidden in Israel.

Perhaps she had become a medium because women in those days had so little power. Or perhaps it seemed an outlet for her helpful nature. But by yielding her soul to spirits, she was abusing herself in the deepest possible way, distorting her dignity as a person for the sake of obtaining power. How fitting that Saul, who had always tried to control the future, spent his last moments consulting her, breaking his own law in the process. Step by step, his insecurities had taken control of him, reducing his soul and disabling his ability to depend on God rather than on himself.

That night the woman of Endor had looked into the eyes of the most powerful man in Israel and had seen the terror there. Did the vision shake her? Did she recognize herself in him? Did her encounter with a true prophet cause her to forsake her trade as a medium? We have no idea what became of her. Sadly, her meeting with Saul marks one of the lowest moments in the life of Israel's first king, revealing his disintegration as a man whose future was destroyed by disobedience.

Saul's tragic ending reminds us that the antidote to fear is always trust. Only faith can cure our worst nightmares, and faith is a gift that is either fed by obedience or starved by disobedience. Forsaking our own desire to manipulate and control people and circumstances, we must trust God to use his power on our behalf.

Her Legacy of Prayer

> *"Do not turn to mediums or seek out spiritists, for you will be defiled by them. I am the LORD your God."*
>
> —*Leviticus 19:31*

REFLECT ON: 1 Samuel 28:3–25.

PRAISE GOD: That he protects us against evil.

OFFER THANKS: That God doesn't hide himself from those
                   who love and follow him.

CONFESS: Any dealings you may have had with the
                   occult: using tarot cards, consulting horo-
                   scopes, visiting fortune-tellers, reading occult
                   books.

ASK GOD: To cleanse and free you from any ill effect of
                   your contact with the occult.

Lift Your Heart

Sometimes we expose ourselves to the occult naively—reading horoscopes in the daily paper, consulting a medium on a whim, or thinking tarot cards simply an innocent game. At other times our interest is more serious, based on a desire for knowledge, healing, or power over others and ourselves. If you have ever dabbled in the occult, now is the time to come clean before God. Express your sorrow and your resolve to follow God by removing from your home anything remotely related to the occult. Confide in your pastor or a mature Christian friend about your involvement, asking them to pray with you as you seek God's protection and forgiveness.

Father, forgive me for my involvement in the occult. I want nothing whatever to do with the realm of evil. Draw me out of the darkness and into the light of your presence. Free me from any lingering effects of my involvement and help me to trust you completely for my future.

22

BATHSHEBA

*Her Name Means "The Seventh Daughter"
or "The Daughter of an Oath"*

HER CHARACTER:	Her beauty made her victim to a king's desire. Though it is difficult to discern her true character, she seems to have found the courage to endure tragedy, winning the king's confidence and eventually securing the kingdom for her son Solomon.
HER SORROW:	To have been molested by a supposedly godly man, who then murdered her husband. To have suffered the loss of one of her sons.
HER JOY:	To have given birth to five sons, one of whom became king of Israel after David's death.
KEY SCRIPTURE:	2 Samuel 11:1–12:25

*B*athsheba squeezed the sponge, moving it rhythmically across her body as though to calm the restless cadence of her thoughts. Normally, she looked forward to the ritual bath marking the end of her monthly period, but tonight the water soothed her skin without refreshing her spirit.

She should be glad for the cool breeze. For flowers. For a lush harvest. But spring could also yield its crop of sorrows, as she well knew. Spring was the season for armies and battles. Once the rains had ceased and the harvest had been gathered, men marched off to war, leaving their women behind.

Bathsheba shivered as she stood up. Though her husband, Uriah, was a seasoned soldier, she still worried about him, wishing she could fall asleep in his arms. But he was camped with the rest of the king's army beneath the open skies of Rabbah, an Ammonite fortress some forty miles northeast of Jerusalem.

The king rose from his bed, unable to sleep. Pacing across the palace roof, he gazed at the city below. Jerusalem seemed calm, a city at peace with itself though at war with its neighbors. Soon his soldiers would gather a great harvest of Ammonite captives, laborers for his expanding kingdom. The casual observer might have thought David a man at peace with his growing power. Instead, the king could not quiet an increasing sense of discontent.

Then, in the half-light, David noticed the figure of a young woman bathing in the walled garden of a house below him. He leaned against the outer edge of the roof for a closer view. Wet hair curling languidly against skin white as lamb's wool. Breasts like rounded apples. He reached as though to steal a touch. Unaware of his gaze, the woman toweled herself dry and stepped into the house. He waited and watched, but even the king could not see through walls.

Over the next few days, David made inquiries and discovered that the vision had a name: she was Bathsheba, the wife of one of his soldiers, Uriah the Hittite. He sent for her. She came to him, he slept with her, and she became pregnant with his child.

Fearing discovery, the king ordered Uriah home from battle. But the soldier surprised him by refusing to spend the night with his wife: "The ark and Israel and Judah are staying in tents, and my lord's men are camped in the open fields. How could I go to my house to eat and drink and lie with my wife? As surely as you live, I will not do such a thing!"

But David convinced Uriah to spend another day in Jerusalem, managing to get him drunk. Surely the wine would overcome his scruples. But it didn't. So David played his last card, entrusting Bathsheba's husband with a letter to Joab, commander of the army. It read: "Put Uriah in the front line where the fighting is fiercest. Then withdraw from him so he will be struck down and die."

So Uriah died by treachery, and David claimed Bathsheba as his wife, her child as his own.

One day, the prophet Nathan approached David, saying: "There were two men in a certain town, one rich and the other poor. The rich man had a very large number of sheep and cattle, but the poor man had nothing except one little ewe lamb he had bought. He raised it, and it grew up with him and his children. It shared his food, drank from his cup, and even slept in his arms. It was like a daughter to him.

"Now a traveler came to the rich man, but the rich man refrained from taking one of his own sheep or cattle to prepare a meal for the traveler who had come to him. Instead, he took the ewe lamb that belonged to the poor man and prepared it for the one who had come to him."

David was incensed: "As surely as the Lord lives, the man who did this deserves to die! He must pay for that lamb four times over, because he did such a thing and had no pity."

Then Nathan said to David, "You are the man! This is what the Lord, the God of Israel, says: 'I anointed you king over Israel, and I delivered you from the hand of Saul. I gave your master's house to you, and your master's wives into your arms. I gave you the house of Israel and Judah. And if all this had been too little, I would have given you even more. Why did you despise the word of the Lord by doing what is evil in his eyes? You struck down Uriah the Hittite with the sword and took his wife to be your own. Now, therefore, the sword will never depart from your house.'"

David's lust for Bathsheba marked the beginning of his long decline. Though God forgave him, he still suffered the consequences of his wrongdoing. His sin was a whirlpool that dragged others into its swirling path. And despite David's prayer and pleading, God allowed the son David had conceived with Bathsheba to die from an illness.

But why did Bathsheba have to suffer along with the man who molested her and murdered her husband? Though the story gives us little insight into her true character, it is hardly likely that Bathsheba was in a position to refuse the king. In Nathan's parable, in fact, she is depicted as an innocent lamb. Why, then, have so many people painted her as a seductress? Perhaps Bathsheba's innocence is too painful to face. That a good person can suffer such tragedies, especially at the hands of a godly person, appalls us. Worse yet, God punishes both David and Bathsheba by taking their son. If we can believe that Bathsheba had an affair with David, we can accept her suffering more easily; her guilt makes David's sin seem less grave and God's punishment less cruel.

Though Bathsheba may not have understood the reasons for her suffering, God gave her favor with King David, making her both a powerful queen and the mother of David's successor, Solomon, who became famous for his great wisdom.

Her Legacy of Prayer

This is what the LORD, the God of Israel says: "I anointed you king over Israel, and I delivered you from the hand of Saul. . . . And if all this had been too little, I would have given you even more. Why did you despise the word of the LORD by doing what is evil in his eyes? You struck down Uriah the Hittite with the sword and took his wife to be your own."

—*2 Samuel 12:7–9*

REFLECT ON: 2 Samuel 12:1–25.

PRAISE GOD: That he is quick to note our suffering.

OFFER THANKS: That God calls the powerful to abide by the same moral standards as the weak.

CONFESS: Any unforgiveness you may have toward
                     another.

ASK GOD: To restore your confidence and to free you
                     from any tendency to take on the mind-set
                     of a victim.

Lift Your Heart

*I*f you have suffered abuse—whether sexual, physical, or emotional—don't bury your feelings, absorbing the shame and guilt that belong to the abuser. Instead, share your pain with at least one other person—a trusted friend or counselor. Find other women who have endured similar abuse and gone on to lead fruitful and significant lives. Determine that you will not let someone else's sin ruin your life. Learn the skills of a survivor. Even if you've never been abused, you probably know someone who has—a daughter, friend, or acquaintance. Do whatever you can to help that person and pray that God will restore her hope.

Father, forgiveness is so hard sometimes. I want justice, not mercy. Please help me to begin the process of forgiveness by letting go of my desire for revenge. Every time I start wishing something negative on those who've hurt me, help me to pray a blessing on their behalf instead. Only you can give me the desire to forgive. Only you can help me do the impossible.

— 23 —

TAMAR, DAUGHTER OF KING DAVID

Her Name Means "Date Tree" or "Palm Tree"

HER CHARACTER:	Tamar shared her father David's good looks. Young and innocent, she was naive to the danger that threatened from her own family.
HER SORROW:	That her half brother saw her only as an object for his lust, destroying her future as a result. And that her father the king did nothing to protect her.
KEY SCRIPTURE:	2 Samuel 13:1–22

David's daughter Tamar was a knockout. No doubt she was destined for a marriage that would strengthen the king's political alliances. Though not under lock and key, she probably lived a rather protected life. But all the precautions in the world couldn't save her from the danger that threatened from David's inner circle.

Amnon was David's heir. As the king's eldest son, he was used to getting his way. But lately he'd grown despondent. Something was bothering him, chasing away his sleep, gnawing at his heart.

One day, Jonadab, David's nephew and Amnon's cousin, asked him: "Why do you, the king's son, look so haggard morning after morning? Won't you tell me?"

Amnon confided in his friend, saying, "I'm in love with Tamar, my brother Absalom's sister."

"Go to bed and pretend to be ill," Jonadab shrewdly advised. "When your father comes to see you, say to him, 'I would like my sister Tamar to come and give me something to eat. Let her prepare the food in my sight so I may watch her and then eat it from her hand.'"

So David, concerned for his son, sent his daughter into a trap that would ruin her life.

After Tamar had prepared a meal for Amnon, he asked her to enter his bedroom and feed him. But as soon as Tamar did, he grabbed her, begging, "Come to bed with me, my sister."

"Don't, my brother!" she said to him. "Don't force me. Such a thing should not be done in Israel! Don't do this wicked thing. What about me? Where could I get rid of my disgrace? And what about you? You would be like one of the wicked fools in Israel. Please speak to the king; he will not keep me from being married to you." But despite her pleas, Amnon forced himself on her.

As soon as the storm of his passion died down, Amnon's infatuation turned to hatred. He threw Tamar out of his house, bolting the door against her, as though she, not he, were the guilty one. Desolate, the young girl tore her robes, throwing ashes on her head and weeping loudly as she wandered the streets. When her brother Absalom found her, he hushed her, saying, "Be quiet now, my sister, he is your brother. Don't take this thing to heart." But Absalom himself took it to heart, hating his half brother Amnon for what he had done.

Though David was furious when he heard the news, he did nothing to punish Amnon. Did he favor his son over his daughter, thinking her hurt a small matter? Or was his moral authority so compromised by his own lust for Bathsheba that he simply couldn't bring himself to confront his eldest son? Whatever the case, Absalom did not share his father's hesitation. Instead, he bided his time, waiting for an opportunity for vengeance, and two years later he murdered Amnon.

First rape, then murder. David's household was devastated not by barbarians outside the gate but by those inside his own family. After Amnon's death, David must have been haunted by Nathan's earlier prophecy after David's own adultery with Bathsheba: "Now, therefore, the sword will never depart from your house. Out of your own household I am going to bring calamity upon you" (2 Samuel 12:10–11). The father's lust was mirrored by the son's; the father's violence by one son's murder of the other.

Tamar, unprotected by her father, betrayed by her own brother, lived in Absalom's house, a desolate woman, without the possibility of marriage or children because she was no longer a virgin. Thus a chain of sin wove its way through David's family, enslaving the innocent along with the guilty.

Her Legacy of Prayer

Though [God] slay me, yet will I hope in him.

—*Job 13:15*

REFLECT ON: 2 Samuel 13:1–31.

PRAISE GOD: For giving us a hope rooted not in the events
                 of this life, but in eternity.

OFFER THANKS: That God has the power to restore our hope.

CONFESS: Any hopelessness about your life.

ASK GOD: To show you that he really does care about you.

Lift Your Heart

Whether we suffer from sexual abuse, the loss of a loved one, divorce, sickness, or financial reverses, we can sometimes feel hopeless about the future. But anyone who belongs to God will not be consigned to a hopeless end. Even if you have difficulty believing this, pray for the grace to want to believe it. As a small gesture expressing your desire, plant a bulb garden in the fall. This simple act will affirm your belief that even after the harshest winter, spring will come again with its profusion of color and new life. If fall is still far away, buy a colorful bouquet to grace your bedside table for the week ahead. Pick up a copy of Judith Couchman's beautiful book *A Garden of Promise*. Just reading her practical and graceful insights about gardening will make you glad.

Father, plant something new in my life, a sprig of hope that will set me on a new course. Help me to live in the present, spending my emotional energies on this moment rather than squandering them on regrets about the past or anxieties about the future.

—— 24 ——
THE WISE WOMAN
OF ABEL

HER CHARACTER:	Rather than passively waiting for someone else to save her city, she had the wisdom and courage to act quickly and decisively.
HER SORROW:	That her city, though faithful to the king, was besieged by his army because it had been infiltrated by a rebellious leader.
HER JOY:	That she was able to successfully intercede for the town, thus averting disaster for many innocent people.
KEY SCRIPTURE:	2 Samuel 20:14–22

⟩⟨

$\mathcal{T}$eddy Roosevelt once said that "nine-tenths of wisdom consists in being wise in time." After the dust settles, the storm clears, the action stops, it's often too late for wisdom to work its marvels.

Many women in Scripture stand out for their wisdom. One woman, who lived in a town at Israel's northern border, is identified solely as "a wise woman" (2 Samuel 20:16), acting quickly to save her city.

The sad stories of Bathsheba and Tamar highlighted the decline of David's household. Eventually, Absalom, David's third son, rebelled and was killed in a battle for the throne. In the midst of this political instability, a rabble-rouser by the name of Sheba, from the tribe of Benjamin

(Saul's tribe), attempted still another revolt. But Joab, the commander of David's army, chased Sheba all the way to Abel Beth Maacah, in the north.

Joab had constructed siege ramps to assault the walls of Abel and squelch the rebellion. It was quite evident to the inhabitants of the city that the entire city might be destroyed unless someone acted quickly to preserve the peace.

Suddenly, a woman stood on the walls of Abel and shouted: "Listen! Listen! Tell Joab to come here so I can speak to him.

"We are the peaceful and faithful in Israel," she cried out. "You are trying to destroy a city that is a mother in Israel. Why do you want to swallow up the Lord's inheritance?" she challenged Joab.

"Far be it from me to swallow up or destroy!" he replied. "A man named Sheba son of Bicri, from the hill country of Ephraim, has lifted up his hand against the king, against David. Hand over this one man, and I'll withdraw from the city."

"His head will be thrown to you from the wall," she shouted back.

The woman turned to her fellow citizens, urging them to act. In just moments, a man's head came careening over the wall. Disaster was averted.

The men in this story appear to behave only in conventional terms: mobilize the army, build a siege ramp, violently smash the city walls, squelch the rebellion. But the woman looked for another solution, one that would keep the peace and spare lives on both sides. Because she acted wisely and well, interceding on behalf of her people, innocent lives on both sides of the city walls were spared.

Her Legacy of Prayer

If you call out for insight and cry aloud for understanding, and if you look for it as for silver and search for it as for hidden treasure, then you will understand the fear of the LORD *and find the knowledge of God. For the* LORD *gives wisdom, and from his mouth come knowledge and understanding.*

—*Proverbs 2:3–6*

REFLECT ON: 2 Samuel 20:16–20.

PRAISE GOD: For his wisdom, which far surpasses anything we might imagine.

OFFER THANKS: That true wisdom has nothing to do with intellectual ability but everything to do with humble dependence on God.

CONFESS: Any laziness that keeps you from searching out God's wisdom for your own life.

ASK GOD: To help you treasure his wisdom so that you are willing to actively seek it out.

Lift Your Heart

Wisdom has nothing to do with how many "gray cells" you possess. You can be smart as a whip but still full of foolishness. Take a few moments to reflect on this condensed and paraphrased passage from the book of Proverbs (3:13–18):

Blessed is the woman who has found wisdom. She has found something more precious than gold. None of her desires can compare with wisdom. For wisdom brings life, wealth, honor, and peace. Wisdom is a tree of life to be gladly embraced.

Here are a few vital suggestions for cultivating wisdom in your life:

• Pray for it, remembering it is a gift from God.
• Read and meditate regularly on Scripture.

- Surround yourself with wise friends—listen and learn from them. (Consider meeting regularly with a spiritual director.)
- Make quick obedience a hallmark of your spiritual life; it leads to wisdom.

_____

Lord, you are the source of the wisdom that brings life, wealth, honor, and peace. May wisdom be like a growing tree in my life, bearing abundant fruit for your kingdom.

25

RIZPAH

Her Name Means
"A Hot Stone or Coal"

HER CHARACTER:	Saul's concubine Rizpah was the mother of Armoni and Mephibosheth. Though a woman with few rights and little power, she displayed great courage and loyalty after the death of her sons.
HER SORROW:	That her only sons were executed and their bodies dishonored because of their father's crime.
HER JOY:	That the bodies of her sons were finally given an honorable burial.
KEY SCRIPTURE:	2 Samuel 21:8–14

$ne day a rabbi stood on a hill overlooking a certain city. The rabbi watched in horror as a band of Cossacks on horseback suddenly attacked the town, killing innocent men, women, and children. Some of the slaughtered were his own disciples. Looking up to heaven, the rabbi exclaimed: "Oh, if only I were God." An astonished student, standing nearby, asked, "But, Master, if you were God, what would you do differently?" The rabbi replied: "If I were God I would do nothing differently. If I were God, I would understand."★

★As told by Joanna Laufer and Kenneth S. Lewis in *Inspired* (New York: Doubleday, 1998), 5.

One day a woman named Rizpah was standing on a hill in Israel, watching the execution of seven men. Her grief was sharp, for among the dead were her own two sons. Executed for their father's crime, their bodies were left to rot on the hillside, despite a law requiring burial by sunset. Perhaps, like the rabbi, Rizpah wished she were God, even for a moment. Maybe then she would understand the "why" of what she had just witnessed.

It is not hard to imagine Rizpah's suffering. To watch as her body convulses in sorrow. To see her pound a fist against her breast to beat away the grief. When will she turn away from the gruesome spectacle? we wonder. But instead of fleeing the scene of her sorrow, she faces it, drawing close to bloodied bodies she once had cradled in her arms. Then she spreads sackcloth on a rock and sits down, refusing to move except to beat off birds of prey by day and jackals by night. Her vigil would last for several months—from mid April to early October. Rizpah would not bury her grief as long as the bodies of her sons remain unburied.

Joshua had promised to live in peace with the Gibeonites, but Saul had murdered many of them during his reign, attempting to annihilate them. As a result of Saul's oath-breaking, Israel suffered a famine for three years running. In retribution, the Gibeonites had asked David for seven of Saul's male offspring. David surrendered Saul's two sons by Rizpah and five grandsons by Saul's daughter Merab. Blood was spilt for blood.

Scripture doesn't say whether Rizpah's sons shared their father's guilt. But like all mothers whose children have perished by violence—those in Bosnia, Kosovo, Rwanda, our own inner cities and even our suburbs—Rizpah must have understood the terrible link between sin and death. One person's sin is a cancer that spreads. By refusing to hide her grief, by living out her anguish in public, Rizpah gave meaning to her sons' deaths, making the entire nation face the evil of what had happened.

Finally, the rains came. Finally, the king's heart was touched. Hearing of Rizpah's loyalty and courage, David ordered the remains of the executed to be buried. He even ordered Saul and his son Jonathan's bones to be reclaimed and buried.

Scripture doesn't say that God ordered David to hand the men over to the Gibeonites in the first place, or even that the famine ended when they were executed. Instead, as Virginia Stem Owens points out in her book *Daughters of Eve*, the Bible indicates that God answered prayers on behalf of the land after the dead were given a decent burial. David's act in honor of the dead may have signaled an end to Israel's divisions. Finally, the land could be healed and the Israelites could reunite under David's leadership.

Rizpah made the people look at the cost of sin. Like many women in ancient cultures, she had few rights and little power. But her persistent courage gave meaning to her sons' deaths and helped a nation deal with the sin of its leader. Her story is tragic, her response memorable. Perhaps because of her, other mothers in Israel were spared a similar grief, at least for a time.

Her Legacy of Prayer

Rizpah daughter of Aiah took sackcloth and spread it out for herself on a rock. From the beginning of the harvest till the rain poured down from the heavens on the bodies, she did not let the birds of the air touch them by day or the wild animals by night.

—*2 Samuel 21:10*

REFLECT ON: 2 Samuel 21:8–14.

PRAISE GOD: For giving mothers the power to love their children so fiercely.

OFFER THANKS: For the way other women have stood by you in times of difficulty.

CONFESS:	Any tendency to back off rather than confront important moral issues with love and courage.
ASK GOD:	To stretch your love beyond your own family circle so that it becomes a force that shapes the world around you.

Lift Your Heart

*M*others are often their children's first line of defense. How tragic when children never experience the power of a mother's protecting love. So many abused children shuffle through our social system with devastating results. So many unborn children perish quietly, with no one to mourn their passing. We cannot save all the motherless children, but we can reach out one at a time. Pray about whether you could become a big sister to a young girl in need. Go out of your way to make a neglected child feel welcome in your home. Speak out against the forces in our culture that devalue human life. Lend your voices to those that clamor for peace in our world. Do what you can where you can. Let your love be fierce and strong. Don't back off.

Father, thank you for the important women in my life. I know your own love better because of how they loved me. Help me become a spiritual mother to those you bring into my life. Make me willing to do what it takes to love them fiercely and well.

26

THE QUEEN
OF SHEBA

HER CHARACTER: A pagan queen, she prized wisdom above
                  power. She appears to have been intellectually
                  gifted, with a good head for business and
                  diplomacy.

HER JOY: That her quest for wisdom was rewarded
                  beyond her expectations.

KEY SCRIPTURES: 1 Kings 10:1–13; Matthew 12:42

$\succ$

Sheba was a fragrant land, famous for its perfumes and spices. Located on the southwestern tip of Arabia, bordering the Red Sea, it traded precious commodities like gold, frankincense, and myrrh to kingdoms in Africa, India, and the Mediterranean. Little wonder that passing caravans brought news of the wide world to Sheba's queen.

Lately, the queen had heard marvelous stories of Solomon, the son of Bathsheba and David, now Israel's third king. At his birth, a prophet had named him "beloved of the Lord." Some said he was the wisest man alive.

The queen smiled as she recalled the tale of the two prostitutes. Both had claimed to be mother to the same infant. How could the king possibly know who was telling the truth and who a lie? But Solomon merely ordered the baby cut in half, to be divided equally between the two women. He knew the real mother would relinquish her rights rather than let her child perish. Indeed, the king's cleverness had quickly unearthed the truth, reuniting the heartbroken mother and her child.

The queen had also heard of the fabulous temple and palace Solomon had built in Jerusalem. Such a ruler, she realized, would have little trouble controlling the international trade routes crisscrossing his kingdom.

Though Jerusalem lay fifteen hundred miles to the north, the queen was determined to see for herself whether Solomon measured up to even half the tales told of him. Perhaps she could also establish a trade agreement with Israel that would ensure Sheba's future prosperity. So she assembled a caravan of camels and loaded them with precious spices, gems, and four-and-a-half tons of gold. Her entrance into Jerusalem would have created an unforgettable spectacle, adding to Solomon's growing fame.

Day after day, the queen pounded Solomon with hard questions. But nothing was too difficult for the king to explain. Her questions finally exhausted, the Queen of Sheba was overwhelmed by what she had discovered: "The report I heard in my own country about your achievements and your wisdom is true. But I did not believe these things until I came and saw with my own eyes. Indeed, not even half was told me; in wisdom and wealth you have far exceeded the report I heard. How happy your men must be! How happy your officials, who continually stand before you and hear your wisdom! Praise be to the Lord your God, who has delighted in you and placed you on the throne of Israel. Because of the Lord's eternal love for Israel, he has made you king, to maintain justice and righteousness."

Then the queen gave Solomon all the gold and spices she had brought with her, perhaps foreshadowing the Magi's gift of gold, frankincense, and myrrh to the Christ Child nearly a thousand years later. In fact, Jesus himself referred to the Queen of Sheba when he replied to the Pharisees who had demanded from him a miraculous sign: "The Queen of the South will rise at the judgment with this generation and condemn it; for she came from the ends of the earth to listen to Solomon's wisdom, and now one greater than Solomon is here."

Though ruler of a pagan nation, the Queen of Sheba was drawn to the wisdom of God. After all, she made an arduous and dangerous journey, traveling three thousand miles round-trip in order to meet the world's wisest man. Surely, she must have thought the price worth paying.

Her Legacy of Prayer

How happy your men must be! How happy your officials, who continually stand before you and hear your wisdom! Praise be to the LORD your God, who has delighted in you and placed you on the throne of Israel! Because of the LORD's eternal love for Israel, he has made you king, to maintain justice and righteousness.

—*1 Kings 10:8–9*

REFLECT ON: 1 Kings 10:1–13.

PRAISE GOD: For his generosity.

OFFER THANKS: For God's wisdom working through others.

CONFESS: Any tendency to trust too much in your own wisdom without seeking godly counsel.

ASK GOD: To pour out wisdom on leaders in the church and in the government so that his ways are honored in your family, community, and nation.

Lift Your Heart

Think about the gifts the Queen of Sheba lavished on Solomon— the perfume, spices, precious stones, and gold—as tangible acknowledgments of his greatness. Yet Solomon was only a man. What can you lavish on the One who is far greater than he? You can be generous with your praise, telling God everything you love about him. You can be generous with your time, going out of your way to help those in need. You can be generous with your trust, acting and praying in a way that shows your confidence in God's goodness and power. You can be generous with your money, giving what you can from your small hoard. This week, don't be stingy. Think of at least one extravagant way to express your awe and your affection for God.

———————

Jesus, everything I've heard about you is true, but I didn't believe it until you showed yourself to me. Then I realized I hadn't been told the half of it. Your wisdom, mercy, power, and kindness exceed everything I've ever heard. How happy are the women who belong to you! I praise the Father for delighting in you and placing you above everything and everyone. Because of the Lord's eternal love, he has made you our King.

— 27 —

JEZEBEL

Her Name Means
"Where Is the Prince?"

HER CHARACTER:	A religious woman, she spread idolatry throughout Israel. Powerful, cunning, and arrogant, she actively opposed God, even in the face of indisputable proofs of his sovereignty.
HER TRIUMPH:	To have enhanced her own power at the expense of others.
HER TRAGEDY:	Her arrogance led to a violent death.
KEY SCRIPTURES:	1 Kings 16:29–33; 18:1–19:2; 21:1–25; 2 Kings 9

Jezebel was a Phoenician princess, daughter of the priest-king of Sidon. Married to King Ahab, she reigned as queen in northern Israel one hundred years after David's death and sixty years after Israel split into northern and southern kingdoms just after Solomon's death.

A woman of great conviction and unwavering devotion, Jezebel's ardent worship was directed not to the God of Israel but to the pagan fertility god Baal, thought to control the rain and hence the harvest. So determined was she to convert Israel to her own religion that she hunted down and killed all the prophets she could lay her hands on, replacing them with 850 of her own.

Despite Jezebel's efforts, one prophet had escaped her, and he was the most annoying of all. His name was Elijah, which meant "My God

Is Yahweh." By contrast, Jezebel meant "Where Is the Prince (Baal)?" or "The Prince (Baal) Exists." Inevitably, the two squared off.

By pushing Baal worship, Jezebel was spreading idolatry across Israel. Despite her considerable efforts, her brand of worship wasn't producing the desired results, for the fields remained barren. The fertility gods, it seemed, were impotent.

Elijah, meanwhile, warned King Ahab: "As the Lord, the God of Israel, lives, whom I serve, there will be neither dew nor rain in the next few years except at my word" (1 Kings 17:1).

Elijah's prophecy came true. Finally, after three-and-a-half years of drought and famine, Elijah challenged the king to assemble the prophets of Baal and Asherah to compete in a lopsided contest—850 to one. Two bulls were prepared for sacrifice, but the fire for sacrifice was not lit. Instead, the true God would prove himself by sending fire from heaven.

From morning until noon Baal's prophets danced and shouted, "O Baal, answer us!" But the god of the storm was silent.

Relishing the spectacle, Elijah couldn't resist a few well-aimed taunts: "Shout louder! Surely he is a god! Perhaps he is deep in thought, or busy, or traveling. Maybe he is sleeping and must be awakened." Elijah's sarcasm spurred the prophets of Baal to more frenzied efforts, but Baal, the god of fire, couldn't even light a match that day.

Then Elijah's turn came. To dramatize the difficulty of his task, he drenched the sacrifice with water not once but three times, praying: "O Lord, God of Abraham, Isaac, and Israel, let it be known today that you are God in Israel and that I am your servant and have done all these things at your command."

Immediately, fire burned up the sacrifice. Rallying the people, Elijah then slaughtered Jezebel's 850 prophets.

Enraged at the news, the queen sent a messenger to Elijah, vowing to kill him. But he fled south, beyond her grasp.

Still, Jezebel kept busy, managing to find other targets for her schemes. One day she discovered her husband, Ahab, in a childish rage.

Pouting, Ahab confided his troubles to her. Naboth, his near neighbor, had a lovely vineyard that the king desired. It would make such a nice vegetable garden. Yet his stingy subject refused to sell it.

"Is this how you act as king over Israel?" Jezebel challenged. "Get up and eat! Cheer up. I'll get you the vineyard."

Jezebel wrote a letter in Ahab's name and sent it to the elders of the town instructing them to produce false witnesses to testify that Naboth had cursed both God and the king, offenses punishable by death.

Ahab felt better when he heard that Naboth had been stoned to death as a traitor. Now his table would be laden with delicious vegetables straight from the garden. But then who should show up but Elijah, interrupting the king's leisurely stroll through his new garden.

"So you have found me, my enemy," the king greeted him.

"I have found you," Elijah replied, "because you have sold yourself to do evil in the eyes of the Lord. I am going to bring disaster on you. I will consume your descendants and cut off from Ahab every last male in Israel—slave or free. And also, concerning Jezebel, the Lord says: 'Dogs will devour Jezebel by the wall of Jezreel.'"

Elijah's words came true. Ahab eventually died in battle, the dogs licking the blood from his chariot. Jezebel, however, survived him by at least ten years. Finally, a man called Jehu came riding into Jezreel one day to carry out the last half of Elijah's prophecy.

Tough as nails, Jezebel stood proudly at the window of her palace. With painted eyes and perfectly coifed hair, she looked every inch the queen. Never one to back away from a challenge, Jezebel seized the initiative, shouting at Jehu: "Have you come in peace, Zimri [the name of a traitor], you murderer of your master?" But Jehu simply ignored her, challenging those who stood near her. "Who is on my side? Throw her down!" Quickly, Jezebel's servants shoved her through the window, watching her body hurtle to the ground. The palace walls were splattered a bloody red as horses trampled her and the palace dogs finished the job. A powerful figure while she lived, hardly anything of her remained just shortly after her death.

Paired with Israel's worst king, Jezebel was the nation's worst queen and one of the Bible's most infamous women. How different her story would have been had she harnessed her power, her drive, and her devotion in the service of God. A strong character, Jezebel could have been a female apostle Paul, whose misguided zeal was redirected toward the kingdom of God. Instead, unlike many biblical figures who are depicted with a mixture of good and bad traits, she stands out as someone purely evil, whose moral character is one-dimensional. Totally devoted to her gods, she reflected their image completely. Despite obvious miracles and repeated warnings, she was a woman who chose to harden her heart and suffer the consequences.

Her Legacy of Prayer

Who knows the power of your anger? For your wrath is as great as the fear that is due you. Teach us to number our days aright, that we may gain a heart of wisdom.

—*Psalm 90:11–12*

REFLECT ON: 2 Kings 9.

PRAISE GOD: That he does not allow evil to go unpunished.

OFFER THANKS: For justice, even when it seems delayed.

CONFESS: Any tendency to take God's mercy for granted.

ASK GOD: To give you a healthy fear of offending him.

Lift Your Heart

Had Jezebel thought more about her inevitable end, her story may have been remarkably different. As much as we like to pretend we're never going to die, it's healthy to consider our own demise from time to time. Doing so humbles us, strips away our illusions, reminds us we are creatures answerable to a Creator. Take thirty minutes to imagine your last day on earth. With whom do you want to spend it? What kind of memories do you want to leave behind? Do you have any lingering regrets, any unfinished business, any unfulfilled dreams? Ask God to guide you through this exercise. Let him show you what in your life can be affirmed and celebrated and what still needs to be transformed by his grace. Then tell him you're willing to do whatever it takes to become the woman he wants you to be.

Lord, I don't want to fear you for the wrong reasons, but for the right ones—to stand in awe because of who you are. Gracious God, let me never make light of your justice or your power. Instead, let me live in a way that honors you. For you are Wonderful Counselor, Mighty God, Everlasting Father, Prince of Peace.

28

THE WIDOW
OF ZAREPHATH

HER CHARACTER:	A foreigner facing starvation, she showed extraordinary hospitality to one of God's prophets, providing a safe harbor for him.
HER SORROW:	To suffer extreme poverty, famine, and the loss of husband and son.
HER JOY:	To experience repeated miracles of God's provision.
KEY SCRIPTURES:	1 Kings 17:8–24; Luke 4:25–26

er arms were spindly and rough, like the dry twigs she had gathered for kindling. Her body shook now as she stood over the fire, greedily sipping and sucking the steam from the pan, as though the smell of frying bread could fill her belly and soothe her fears. She had lived her life a stone's throw from the Mediterranean, at Zarephath, seven miles south of Sidon, in a territory ruled by Jezebel's father. She had always loved the sea, but now its watery abundance only mocked her, reminding her of all she lacked.

Tears escaped her eyes, try as she might to blink them back. How hard it was to suffer her fears alone, to wake in the night with no one to warm her, no one to whisper sweet lies about tomorrow. If only her husband were alive to squeeze a harvest from the fields. But he had died before the drought, leaving her with a small son, a house, and little else. Every night she hoped for rain, but every morning her depression deepened as she woke to a brilliant sky.

Though she starved herself to feed her child, his distended belly accused her. His need condemned her. She had failed in the most basic ways a mother could, unable to protect, nurture, and provide. These days she stood with shoulders hunched as though to hide her breasts. Today she had scraped the last bit of flour from the barrel and poured the last drop of oil from the jug. She began to prepare a final supper for herself and her child.

But then a stranger had called to her: "Would you bring me a little water in a jar so I may have a drink?"

Graciously, she had gone to fetch it, only to have him call after her, "And bring me, please, a piece of bread."

Was the man mad? she wondered. He might as well ask her to snap her fingers and produce a cow for slaughter.

She turned on her heel and replied, "As surely as the Lord your God lives, I don't have any bread—only a handful of flour in a jar and a little oil in a jug. I am gathering a few sticks to take home and make a meal for myself and my son, that we may eat it—and die."

But the man had persisted. "Don't be afraid. Go home and do as you have said. But first make a small cake of bread for me from what you have and bring it to me and then make something for yourself and your son. For this is what the Lord, the God of Israel, says: 'The jar of flour will not be used up and the jug of oil will not run dry until the day the Lord gives rain on the land.'"

Instead of cursing the stranger for his callousness, as we might expect, the woman did exactly as he had requested, feeding him the food she had reserved for herself and her son.

The woman from Zarephath wasn't a Jew, but a Phoenician. She had no idea that the stranger was Elijah, a prophet who had the gall to inform King Ahab that God was withholding rain to punish Israel's idolatry. She would have been astonished to learn that this same God had instructed Elijah to "go at once to Zarephath of Sidon and stay there. I have commanded a widow in that place to supply you with food."

The widow of Zarephath had felt utterly alone, not knowing God had his eye on her. Yet for some reason she believed Elijah and acted accordingly, giving him everything she had in the world.

After that, every time she dipped her hand into the flour, every time she poured oil from the jug, the widow saw another miracle unfold, another sign of favor, additional evidence of God's provision. Just as Elijah had promised, the supply of flour and oil lasted day after day, month after month, never failing until at last the rains came and revived the land.

How like God to construct a parable of grace during a time of judgment, to display his mercy and power in the midst of weakness and need. The widow's faith saved not only her son and herself but actually provided a refuge for Elijah, who may have wondered why God chose such flimsy protection—a destitute woman who lived in the territory of his worst enemy, Jezebel.

The widow's faith would be tested again when her young son later died. But she would also be the first woman to witness God's power to raise the dead, which he did in response to Elijah's repeated prayers on behalf of her child. A woman who endured extreme difficulties, her story reveals God's power to provide what we need the most—a commodity of the heart called faith.

Her Legacy of Prayer

Then the woman said to Elijah, "Now I know that you are a man of God and that the word of the LORD from your mouth is the truth."
—*1 Kings 17:24*

REFLECT ON: 1 Kings 17:8–24.

PRAISE GOD: For his constant attentiveness.

OFFER THANKS: For all the ways God has already provided for you and for the ways he will provide in the future.

CONFESS: Any tendency to act as though God really doesn't care about what's happening to you.

ASK GOD: To make you a woman who relies on him daily for her physical, emotional, and spiritual needs.

Lift Your Heart

Whenever we spin anxious scenarios about the future, we waste precious emotional energy. This kind of worrying represents a negative use of the power of our imagination. As such, it can be a misguided attempt to control the future. But instead of controlling the future, we soon discover that anxiety controls us. Jesus said, "Do not worry about tomorrow, for tomorrow will worry about itself. Each day has enough trouble of its own" (Matthew 6:34). Begin to form habits that will help you break the power of worry in your life. Start by thanking God each morning for some small sign of his goodness: a loving friend, a beautiful garden, a child's smile. Gratitude will increase your sense of God's presence in your life. Then, set aside some time to think about ways God has taken care of you in the past. Write them down and make them part of your faith arsenal, so that when you are tempted by anxious thoughts you can remind yourself of concrete examples of how God has already provided for you.

Father, how easy it is to let anxiety snuff out my gratitude. Help me to linger thankfully in your presence rather than simply rushing on to my next desperate request. Use my weakness and need as a showcase for your strength.

29

THE SHUNAMMITE WOMAN

HER CHARACTER:	Generous and hospitable, she was a wealthy and capable woman who showed great kindness to one of God's prophets.
HER SORROW:	To lose the son that had been promised her.
HER JOY:	To experience just how deep God's faithfulness goes.
KEY SCRIPTURES:	2 Kings 4:8–37; 2 Kings 8:1–6

Just a few miles north of Jezreel, where Jezebel's story had drawn to its grim conclusion, lived a wealthy Jewish woman whose sharp eye kept track of travelers from Nazareth to Jerusalem. One of the more colorful characters who frequented the road outside her house was Elisha, the prophet who succeeded Elijah.

One day the Shunammite woman invited Elisha to linger for a meal. Afterward, she said to her husband, "Let's make a small room on the roof and put in it a bed and a table, a chair and a lamp for him. Then he can stay there whenever he comes to us."

Moved by her kindness, Elisha inquired, through his servant Gehazi, whether he could use his influence with Israel's king on her behalf. But the woman wasn't looking for favors at court, so Elisha pressed his servant, saying, "What can be done for her?"

Gehazi merely pointed out the obvious: the woman and her aging husband were childless, without an heir to carry on the family name.

So Elisha summoned the woman and made an incredible promise: "About this time next year you will hold a son in your arms."

"No, my lord," she objected. "Don't mislead your servant, O man of God!"

Yet, a year later, just as Elisha had foretold, the woman held a squalling infant in her arms, laughing as she told others the story of God's surprising gift. Unlike so many of her female forebears—Sarah, Rebekah, Rachel, Tamar, Hannah—the Shunammite woman seemed content without children. Elisha's promise, however, was an arrow homing straight to its target, fulfilling the unspoken desire of her heart.

One morning a few years later, a servant entered the house with the little boy in his arms, explaining that the child had complained of a headache while visiting his father in the fields. Perhaps he had lingered too long in the sun.

The boy's face was flushed, his forehead hot as his mother caressed it, hushing him with soothing sounds and songs. But despite murmured words of reassurance, she felt her own fear spreading. The tighter she held him, the more his spirit seemed to retreat. His breathing was labored, his eyes listless. At about noon he died.

Without a word, she carried his small body to the prophet's room, laying it tenderly on Elisha's bed. Closing the door, she summoned a servant and left immediately for Mount Carmel, where she hoped to find Elisha.

Spotting her in the distance, the prophet wondered aloud what could prompt her to make the twenty-five-mile journey north. "Run to meet her," he urged Gehazi, "and ask, 'Are you all right? Is your husband all right? Is your child all right?'"

But the woman merely brushed Gehazi aside with polite words and rushed straight to Elisha, exclaiming: "Did I ask you for a son, my lord? Didn't I tell you, 'Don't raise my hopes'?"

Immediately the prophet instructed Gehazi: "Tuck your cloak into your belt, take my staff in your hand, and run. If you meet anyone, do not greet him, and if anyone greets you, do not answer. Lay my staff on the boy's face."

The woman, however, wasn't about to settle for a stand-in. So the prophet hurried to Shunem just behind Gehazi, who had gone on ahead to carry out his master's orders. When Elisha arrived, he found the boy lying quiet and cold on his couch. Elisha closed the door behind him. Praying, he stretched his body across the boy's so that hands, mouth, and eyes touched. As he lay there, he could feel the chilled body warming beneath him. He got up and paced the room for a while. At last he stretched himself across the lifeless body again and prayed. The boy's chest lifted. Then he sneezed! Then sneezed again. Death was cheated of its prize.

The Shunammite woman may, in fact, have heard the story of how Elijah had raised the son of the widow of Zarephath in similar circumstances. If so, that miracle would certainly have fueled her hope, giving her the courage to seek her own miracle rather than collapse under so great a weight of grief. Now, as she saw for herself the irrefutable sign of God's loving-kindness, she fell at Elisha's feet and bowed to the ground. God had been true to his word, fulfilling his promise to her and then preserving it in the face of impossible circumstances.

Her Legacy of Prayer

"About this time next year," Elisha said, "you will hold a son in your arms."
—*2 Kings 4:16*

REFLECT ON: 2 Kings 4:8–37.

PRAISE GOD: That he never overlooks even a small kindness performed out of love for him.

OFFER THANKS: For the kindness you have experienced at the hands of others.

CONFESS: Your tendency to overlook others' needs because you are so focused on your own.

ASK GOD: To make you jealous for opportunities to care for others in basic and practical ways.

Lift Your Heart

The Shunammite woman is a wonderful example of someone who anticipated Jesus' words to his disciples to "seek first his [the Father's] kingdom and his righteousness, and all these things will be given to you as well" (Matthew 6:33). Like the lilies of the field, she didn't worry about God's provision and so experienced it abundantly. Ask for an opportunity this week to perform an act of practical kindness or hospitality for someone else. Consider lending your prayers, your gifts, and your energy on a regular basis to a group or ministry working to bring justice to those most in need of it.

Father, show me someone's need today. Then help me break out of my own small world and find a way to show your love to that person.

30

ATHALIAH AND JEHOSHEBA

ATHALIAH

Her Name Means
"The Lord Is Great"

HER CHARACTER:	Granddaughter of Omri, one of Israel's most idolatrous and evil kings, she was the daughter of Ahab and most likely of Jezebel as well. She was the only woman to rule over Judah. While Ahab and Jezebel spread Baal worship in the northern kingdom of Israel, Athaliah was busy promoting it a few years later in the southern kingdom of Judah. Driven by her need for power, she murdered her own family members to secure it.
HER TRIUMPH:	That her ruthlessness paid off, at least for a time, making her the ruler of Judah.
HER DISAPPOINTMENT:	That her attempt to destroy the royal line of Judah failed.
KEY SCRIPTURES:	2 Kings 11; 2 Chronicles 22; 23:11–21

JEHOSHEBA

Her Name Means
"Swear by His Name"

HER CHARACTER:	A princess and the wife of the high priest, she was a courageous woman whose actions preserved the line of Judah, from which the Messiah would come.
HER SORROW:	To have endured Athaliah's reign in Judah and to have suffered the loss of many of her nephews at the queen's hand.
HER JOY:	To have preserved the life of her brother's youngest son, Joash, so that he could become the rightful king of Judah.
KEY SCRIPTURES:	2 Kings 11:2; 2 Chronicles 22:11

Wicked queens are the stuff of fairy tales. Remember the Snow Queen in the tale by Hans Christian Andersen, or the evil queen in *The Lion, the Witch and the Wardrobe*? Athaliah was at least as bad as her fairy-tale counterparts, a queen who chilled the hearts of God's people by murdering her own grandsons and promoting Baal worship in the southern kingdom of Judah, just as her parents, Ahab and Jezebel, had promoted it in the north.

Athaliah married the king of Judah, thereby cementing an alliance between the northern and southern kingdoms. But after a few years he died and was succeeded by Athaliah's son, Ahaziah. In just a few months, Jehu, Jezebel's nemesis, slaughtered the new king.

After Queen Athaliah's husband and son were killed, she must have felt vulnerable and isolated, doubly so since her father Ahab's line had also been destroyed in Israel. Her paranoia and lust for power formed a toxic mixture, moving her to murder her own grandchildren to secure Judah's throne for herself. Indeed she may even have gloated that she, Baal's emissary, had snuffed out Judah's royal heirs, making it impossible for God to fulfill his promise of a future Messiah from David's line in the tribe of Judah.

For a few years, from about 841–835 B.C., Athaliah reigned in Judah, promoting Baal worship and leading the people further and further from God. But right under her nose a conspiracy was taking shape. One of her grandsons still lived. Her own stepdaughter, Jehosheba, had hidden the infant, Joash, before the queen could murder him along with Ahaziah's other sons. Married to the high priest, Jehosheba risked her life by tucking the royal heir away in the temple for six years. Then, when the boy turned seven, her husband arranged a coup, crowning young Joash king.

As soon as Athaliah caught wind of the plot, she rushed to the temple, tearing her robes and screaming, "Treason! Treason!" But as had happened with her mother, Jezebel, before her, no one paid the slightest attention. Instead, Queen Athaliah was promptly seized and executed just outside the temple. As soon as the queen was killed, the people of Judah celebrated by destroying the temple of Baal and its chief priest.

While the comparisons between Athaliah and Jezebel are all too obvious, their story reminds us of another that took place seven hundred years before. Egypt's Pharaoh, determined to destroy God's people, had ordered every male baby drowned in the Nile River. Like Pharaoh, hoodwinked by one of his own children (his daughter saved Moses and raised him as her own), Athaliah was fooled by her stepdaughter, Jehosheba. Once again a woman's courage and compassion helped to subvert evil and keep the promise alive.

Their Legacy of Prayer

> *But Jehosheba, the daughter of King Jehoram, took Joash son of Ahaziah and stole him away from among the royal princes who were about to be murdered and put him and his nurse in a bedroom. Because Jehosheba, the daughter of King Jehoram and wife of the priest Jehoiada, was Ahaziah's sister, she hid the child from Athaliah so she could not kill him.*
>
> *—2 Chronicles 22:11*

REFLECT ON: 2 Chronicles 22:10–12; 23.

PRAISE GOD: For his power, which is far greater than the power of evil.

OFFER THANKS: That God always does what he says he will no matter the odds against him.

CONFESS: Any tendency to allow difficult circumstances to suffocate your faith.

ASK GOD: For courage to act on behalf of the innocent regardless of consequences.

Lift Your Heart

Scripture often yields its richest insights once you learn to slow down and pray through what you have just read. Use the story of Jehosheba to teach yourself how to pray the Scriptures. Though a minor character, overlooked by most readers, she played a decisive role in the life of God's people. Put yourself in her shoes for just fifteen minutes. Imagine what she must have felt like, not for a moment, but for several years as she defied an evil and powerful queen. Where did she find the strength? What were her temptations and fears? Let your imagination help you envision what her life might have been like. Ask God to speak to you through her story. Then ask for the grace to be like her—to be a woman who always cherishes, protects, and nurtures life. After you've done that, take a moment to think about Jehosheba's joy the moment she learned of Athaliah's final defeat, realizing that the boy whose life she saved was now her king. Let another woman's story encourage you to do what is right regardless of the risks involved.

———————————

Lord, when I am faced with evil, whether it is in government, in the church, or in my neighborhood or family, help me to do whatever is in my power to resist. Give me wisdom to know what to do, courage to act well, and grace to trust you for the outcome.

— 31 —
HULDAH
Her Name Means "Weasel"

HER CHARACTER:	Trusted by the king with a matter of great importance, she was a prophetess whose word generated a significant religious reform.
HER SORROW:	That God's people refused to respond to him with loving obedience, ignoring repeated warnings about the consequences of their unfaithfulness.
HER JOY:	As a prophetess, she was privileged to be a messenger of God.
KEY SCRIPTURES:	2 Kings 22:14–20; 2 Chronicles 34:22–33

She pressed the leather scroll against her breast, as though cradling a living being. The high priest, Hilkiah, and several other men of Jerusalem stood before her. King Josiah wanted to know—would the words of the Book of the Law, which Hilkiah had just discovered in the temple, come to pass?

Holding the scroll by its wooden handles, she unrolled it carefully and began reading:

"Hear, O Israel: The Lord our God, the Lord is one. Love the Lord your God with all your heart and with all your soul and with all your strength. . . . Fear the Lord your God, serve him only and take your oaths in his name. Do not follow other gods, the gods of the peoples around you; for the Lord your God, who is among you, is a jealous God and his anger will burn against you, and he will destroy you from the face of the land (Deuteronomy 6:4–5, 13–15).

"Cursed in the city and cursed in the country . . . sudden ruin because of the evil you have done in forsaking him . . . wasting disease . . . madness, blindness and confusion . . . an object of scorn and ridicule to all the nations . . . because you did not obey the Lord your God" (Deuteronomy 28).

Though her voice was steady, Huldah's throat felt sore from the effort of speaking such words aloud, terrible threats that made her eyes well over, warnings that spawned vision upon vision from the past. In her mind, she watched as Judah's kings Ahaz and Manasseh sacrificed their sons to pagan deities. She saw the smoke of incense rising before pagan idols in the temple. She looked on as prophets were murdered, as diviners and sorcerers were honored, as kings bowed down to the stars and the people followed suit, prostituting themselves to false gods and spurning the advances of the Almighty. She saw the children of Israel marching in chains from the land of milk and honey. Her face flushed as a burning sensation rushed through her body and searing words spilled from her lips:

"This is what the Lord says: 'I am going to bring disaster on this place and its people, according to everything written in the book the king of Judah has read. Because they have forsaken me and burned incense to other gods and provoked me to anger by all the idols their hands have made, my anger will burn against this place and will not be quenched.' Tell the king of Judah, who sent you to inquire of the Lord: 'Because your heart was responsive and you humbled yourself before the Lord when you heard what I have spoken against this place and its people, that they would become accursed and laid waste, and because you tore your robes and wept in my presence, I have heard you, declares the Lord. Therefore I will gather you to your fathers, and you will be buried in peace. Your eyes will not see all the disaster I am going to bring on this place.'"

Huldah is one of only four women with an authentic prophetic ministry mentioned in the Old Testament (along with Miriam, Deborah, and Isaiah's wife). Though prophets like Jeremiah and Zephaniah were also active at the time, King Josiah consulted Huldah about the amazing discovery of the Book of the Law (material that probably forms the core of the book of Deuteronomy).

Beyond the brief scene, imaginatively retold above, we know little of her story—only that God entrusted her with his Word in a time of national crisis. A hundred years earlier, Judah had witnessed God's punishment of the northern kingdom. Faithless Israel had been led captive to Assyria, just as the prophets had warned. Huldah surely knew the sordid details. She could not have missed its frightening significance for Judah. She may also have endured part of Manasseh's fifty-five-year reign, the longest and worst of any king in Judah. Certainly, she would have been heartened by the recent reforms of King Josiah—his attempts to restore the temple though the people had all but forgotten God.

But her words of prophecy confirmed the king's fear. Judah was standing on the edge of judgment. God was a jealous lover who blessed those who loved and obeyed him and cursed those who didn't. Across the centuries, his slow anger was building to a fiery crescendo. Judah's infidelities had not gone unnoticed.

After Huldah's prophecy, Josiah led one of the greatest religious reforms in history, purging Judah and even parts of Israel of paganism. But the kings who followed him soon reversed course, leading the people astray once again. Thirty-five years after Huldah's prophecy, Judah was taken in chains to Babylon and all of its cities were destroyed.

The magnificent kingdom of David and Solomon had come to its end. But though every other nation captured by Assyria and Babylon ceased to exist, Israel still had a future. Chastened, it was never destroyed. Disciplined, it was never forsaken. All because God still loved his people. The words of Isaiah, a prophet who preceded Huldah by a few years, proclaimed a future day of restoration: "They will rebuild the ancient ruins and restore the places long devastated; they will renew the ruined cities. . . . Instead of their shame my people will receive a double portion, and instead of disgrace they will rejoice in their inheritance" (Isaiah 61:4, 7).

Judgment and mercy, law and grace, punishment and salvation—these are the tensions that characterize the story of God's love affair with his people. Huldah was a woman who understood the paradox and who was not afraid to proclaim the truth, even to a king. Her words must have cost her, but she spoke them anyway. She cherished God's Word in a time of spiritual crisis.

Her Legacy of Prayer

When the king heard the words of the Law, he tore his robes. . . . "Go and inquire of the LORD for me and for the remnant in Israel and Judah about what is written in this book that has been found."
—*2 Chronicles 34:19, 21*

REFLECT ON: 2 Chronicles 34:14–33.

PRAISE GOD: For speaking clearly about what he expects from us.

OFFER THANKS: That he gave us his Word in the Bible.

CONFESS: Any complacency in the face of God's commandments.

ASK GOD: For the grace to take his Word seriously so that you understand the connection between love and obedience.

Lift Your Heart

*E*very woman knows the pleasure of a clean house, where floors are thoroughly scrubbed and waxed, windows shined, and cobwebs routed from every nook and cranny. Our hearts can become sullied by daily wear and tear, by disobedience and disregard for doing things God's way. Set aside a day to conduct a little spring-cleaning of your soul. How well have you been doing on the basics—the Ten Commandments?

Check Deuteronomy 5:6–21 for a review in case you've forgotten the commandments or are unfamiliar with them. Don't be so literal in your reading of them that you forget idolatry can take the form of cherishing money, power, or even a person more than you love God. Have you ever murdered someone with hateful words? Have you ever stolen someone's reputation through envy? As you become conscious of your failings, don't wallow in them. Simply admit your sin, asking God's forgiveness and the grace to change. Ask him to make your heart an attractive place for his indwelling presence. Then enjoy his forgiveness and take hold of his grace.

Father, may I have ears to hear your Word and a heart to obey it. Cleanse me from my sin and wash me until I am whiter than snow. Make my soul clean and pure, a broad and spacious place for your indwelling Spirit.

32

ESTHER

Her Name May Derive from "Ishtar,"
the Babylonian Goddess of Love,
or from the Persian Word for "Star"
Her Hebrew Name, "Hadassah," Means "Myrtle"

HER CHARACTER:	An orphan in a foreign land, she displayed great courage in the midst of a crisis. Prior to risking her life for her people, she humbled herself by fasting, and then put her considerable beauty, social grace, and wisdom in the service of God's plan.
HER SORROW:	To learn that her husband, the king, had unwittingly placed her life and the life of her people in jeopardy.
HER JOY:	To watch mourning turn to celebration once the Jews enjoyed relief from their enemies.
KEY SCRIPTURE:	Esther 1–10

ℛ

ashti, queen of Persia, was the most powerful woman in the Middle East, yet her power was as fragile as a candle in a storm. Her husband, Xerxes, had just summoned her to appear before a festive gathering of his nobles. Vashti, however, had no intention of parading herself like a prized cow in front of a herd of drunken men, and refused.

What should be done to punish her insolence? One of the king's counselors spoke for all: "Queen Vashti has done wrong, not only against the king but also against all the nobles and the peoples of all the provinces of King Xerxes. For the queen's conduct will become known to all the women, and so they will despise their husbands and say, 'King Xerxes commanded Queen Vashti to be brought before him, but she would not come.' There will be no end of disrespect and discord."

So poor Vashti bore the brunt of every man's fears. She who had refused the royal summons was forever banished from the royal presence, and a great domestic uprising was squelched before it even began.

After a while, a search was conducted for a new queen to replace Vashti. It so happened that many Jews were living in Persia at the time. Exiled from Judah a hundred years earlier (after Jerusalem's fall in 587 B.C.), they had been deported to Babylon, which in turn was conquered by Persia. Mordecai and his orphaned cousin Esther were among those living in exile, 650 miles northeast of Jerusalem.

Like many other young virgins, the beautiful Esther was gathered into the king's harem. To refuse the privilege may well have meant her death. Counseled by Mordecai to keep her Jewish origins a secret, she spent the next twelve months awaiting her tryst with the king. When the moment came, Esther so pleased Xerxes that she became queen in Vashti's place.

Some time later, an Amalekite named Haman rose to power in Persia. Haman was so highly placed that other officials knelt before him as a sign of respect. One man, however, the Jew Mordecai, refused to kneel. Haman became so angry that he decided to eliminate every Jew in the kingdom.

To ascertain the most favorable moment for destroying them, Haman piously consulted his gods by casting lots (or *pur*). A date eleven months into the future was revealed. Haman immediately persuaded Xerxes to issue a decree that all the Jews in his realm were to be slaughtered on that day. By way of incentive, the decree proclaimed that anyone who killed a Jew could plunder his possessions.

Mordecai reacted immediately by contacting Esther and asking her to beg Xerxes for mercy. But Esther was afraid and replied, "For any man or woman who approaches the king in the inner court without being summoned the king has but one law: that he be put to death. The only exception to this is for the king to extend the gold scepter to him and spare his life. But thirty days have passed since I was called to go to the king."

Mordecai replied, "Do not think that because you are in the king's house you alone of all the Jews will escape. For if you remain silent at this time, relief and deliverance for the Jews will arise from another place, but you and your father's family will perish. And who knows but that you have come to royal position for such a time as this?"

So Esther instructed Mordecai, "Go, gather together all the Jews who are in Susa, and fast for me. Do not eat or drink for three days, night or day. I and my maids will fast as you do. When this is done, I will go to the king, even though it is against the law. And if I perish, I perish."

On the third day, Esther approached the king. As soon as Xerxes saw her, he held out the golden scepter. "What is it, Queen Esther?" he asked. "What is your request? Even up to half the kingdom, it will be given to you."

But Esther merely invited the king and Haman to join her that evening for a banquet she had prepared especially for them. That evening the king again pressed her to ask for whatever she desired, but Esther simply invited the king and Haman to another banquet, to be held the following night. That evening, on his way home, Haman caught sight of Mordecai, sitting smugly rather than kneeling as he passed by. Haman was outraged, but his wife consoled him by proposing an evil scheme—he need merely build a gallows and then ask the king to hang Mordecai on it the next morning.

While Haman was happily constructing a gallows for his enemy, the king was pacing the royal bedroom. Unable to sleep, he ordered one of his servants to read from the annals of the kingdom. That evening's reading just happened to be about how Mordecai had once saved the king's life by warning of a plot against him. It struck the king that Mordecai had never been properly rewarded for his loyalty.

So the next morning the king asked Haman, "What should be done for the man the king delights to honor?"

Assuming the king intended to reward him in some new and marvelous way, the foolish Haman replied with a grandiose suggestion: "For the man the king delights to honor, have them bring a royal robe the king has worn and a horse the king has ridden. Then let one of the king's most noble princes robe the man and lead him on the horse through the city streets, proclaiming before him, 'This is what is done for the man the king delights to honor!'"

"Go at once," the king commanded him. "Get the robe and the horse and do just as you have suggested for Mordecai the Jew."

The man who had planned to bury his enemy was suddenly forced to exalt him that very day!

That night, as the king and Haman were once again drinking wine at the queen's banquet, the king implored Esther to ask for whatever her heart desired. This time she spoke without hesitation: "If I have found favor with you, O king, and if it pleases your majesty, grant me my life—this is my petition. And spare my people—this is my request. For I and my people have been sold for destruction and slaughter and annihilation."

"Where is the man who has dared to do such a thing?" the king demanded.

"The adversary and enemy is this vile Haman."

And so Haman's star, which had risen to so great a height, fell suddenly, like a bolt of lightning crashing from the sky. He was hanged on the very same gallows he had built for the Jew Mordecai, and all his property was given to Esther. Furthermore, the king, because he could not revoke one of his own edicts, issued another to counteract the first one. It gave Jews throughout the empire the right to protect themselves, to destroy and plunder every enemy who might raise a hand against them.

As news of the king's edict spread, many people from various nationalities became so terrified that they claimed to be Jews themselves. The very day Haman's gods had revealed as a day of reckoning for the Jews became a day of reckoning for their enemies. Ever after, the Jews commemorated these events with the Feast of Purim. As the book of Esther says, these days were celebrated "as the time when the Jews got relief from their enemies, and as the month when their sorrow was turned into joy and their mourning into a day of celebration."

Subject to foreign powers after the Exile, God's people must have felt among the weakest elements of society. But weaker even than a Jewish man exiled to a foreign land was a Jewish woman. And weakest of all would have been a young orphan girl of Jewish descent. God had once again employed one of his favorite methods for accomplishing his purposes: He had raised the weakest of the weak, placing her in a position of immense strategic importance.

But it had been up to Esther to decide whether she would play the part God offered. Like Moses, she chose to identify with God's people even if it meant risking her life to do so. And even though exile was a punishment for Israel's long unfaithfulness, God showed that he was still with his people, delivering and protecting them in surprising ways, turning the table on their enemies through a series of stunning reversals. Earthly powers were at work to kill and destroy, but a heavenly power, far greater in scope, was at work to save and preserve.

Her Legacy of Prayer

"For if you remain silent at this time, relief and deliverance for the Jews will arise from another place, but you and your father's family will perish. And who knows but that you have come to royal position for such a time as this?"

—*Esther 4:14*

REFLECT ON: Esther 5–8.

PRAISE GOD: That he turns the wisdom and the power of
                   the world on its head, often using the most
                   surprising tactics to accomplish his plan.

OFFER THANKS: That God has an important purpose for your
                   life.

CONFESS: Any tendency to view your life in isolation
                   from God's people, to shrink back from some
                   step of faith God may be calling you to take.

ASK GOD: For the grace to act courageously and wisely.

Lift Your Heart

*M*any Jewish girls celebrate the Feast of Purim by dressing up as
Queen Esther. One way we can emulate her today is by fasting. Before
Esther took action, she employed a time-honored spiritual discipline
to expose her need before God. Fasting was a visible sign of her
dependency and weakness, an eloquent form of begging God's help.
This week, do a little eloquent begging yourself by choosing a day to
fast from breakfast and lunch—dinner, too, if you're brave! Drink only
water or fruit juice. Perhaps you have a particular need or problem you
would like to surrender to God. Tell God that you need him more than
you need food. Don't try to manipulate him by your self-sacrifice, but
simply allow your weakness to emerge in his presence.

----

*Lord, I need you so much more than food or water. Without your pres-
ence, your protection, your wisdom, your gift of faith, I would be lost.
I'm hungry for you alone. Hear my prayer and give me everything I
need to do your will. Use me in the church and the world around me
to accomplish your purposes.*

33

THE WOMAN
OF PROVERBS 31

HER CHARACTER:	She represents the fulfillment of a life lived in wisdom.
HER JOY:	To be praised by her husband and children as a woman who surpasses all others.
KEY SCRIPTURE:	Proverbs 31:10–31

*P*roverbs brims with less-than-glowing descriptions of women. There are wayward wives, prostitutes, women with smoother-than-oil lips, strange women, loud women, defiant women, wives who are like a continual drip on a rainy day or decay in their husbands' bones, women whose feet never stay home, brazen-faced women, and even a woman so repulsive she is likened to a gold ring in a pig's snout!

Any woman reading Proverbs may be tempted to conclude that its authors tended to blame women for weaknesses actually rooted in the male psyche, especially when it comes to sexual sin. But to balance things out there are also some odious descriptions of men, including scoundrels, villains, chattering fools, and sluggards. And Proverbs actually opens and closes with positive portrayals of women: first as wisdom personified and then as a woman who can do no wrong.

Just who was this woman on a pedestal described in Proverbs 31? Was she, as many think, the ideal wife and mother? In traditional Jewish homes, husbands and children recited the poem in Proverbs 31 at the Sabbath table. Written as an acrostic, each line begins with a Hebrew

153

letter in alphabetical sequence, making it easy to memorize. The poem describes a wealthy, aristocratic woman with a large household to direct. She was hard-working, enterprising, capable, strong, wise, skilled, generous, thoughtful of others, dignified, God-fearing, serene—a tremendous credit to her husband. She arose while it was still dark to feed her family. She looked at a field, considered its merits, and purchased it. She wove cloth and made linen garments, which she then sold. "Her children arise and call her blessed; her husband also, and he praises her: 'Many women do noble things, but you surpass them all'" (verses 28–29).

The description of the woman in Proverbs 31 offers a refreshing contrast to other ancient depictions of women, which tend to portray them in more frivolous and decorative terms, emphasizing only their charm or beauty. Still, the perfect woman of Proverbs 31 hasn't always been a friend to ordinary women. In fact, she has sometimes been rubbed into the faces of lesser women by critical husbands and preachers unable to resist the temptation. What woman could ever measure up to her? And is a woman's worth to be measured only by what she can accomplish in the domestic sphere? Or is the woman in Proverbs 31 a symbol of all the contributions a woman could make within the culture of her day? Regardless of how you answer these questions, there is more to her story than simply being the ideal wife and mother.

Before we can discover more about the Proverbs 31 woman, it is worth posing a broader question: Are there really all that many women running around in the pages of Proverbs? Perhaps, in fact, there are only two main women in Proverbs: the wise woman and the woman of folly (as some have called her). The latter encompasses the adulteress and her many wicked counterparts; the former encompasses wisdom in the abstract and wisdom made concrete in the woman of Proverbs 31.

In Proverbs 3:13–16 a young man is instructed: "Blessed is the man who finds wisdom, the man who gains understanding, for she is more profitable than silver and yields better returns than gold. She is more precious than rubies; nothing you desire can compare with her. Long life is in her right hand; in her left hand are riches and honor." Here is wisdom in the abstract, personified as a woman.

Proverbs 31 echoes this praise: "A wife of noble character who can find? She is worth far more than rubies.... She brings him good, not harm, all the days of her life. She selects wool and flax and works with eager hands. She is like the merchant ships, bringing her food from afar. She gets up while it is still dark; she provides food for her family and portions for her servant girls. She considers a field and buys it; out of her earnings she plants a vineyard" (verses 10, 12–16). Here is a concrete example of what wisdom looks like in a person's life.

By contrast, the man who welcomes the brazen-faced woman, the prostitute, the adulteress is nothing but a fool. He has fallen prey to the woman of folly, who offers deceitful pleasures that will lead to his death.

From beginning to end, Proverbs is a practical handbook for leading a life based on wisdom. In the end, there are only two choices for both men and women: to embrace wisdom or to love folly. The woman of Proverbs 31 may well be meant to inspire both men and women with a picture of what a virtuous life, male or female, is capable of producing: shelter for others, serenity, honor, prosperity, generosity, confidence about the future—true blessedness. Who wouldn't want to be like such a woman? Who wouldn't sing her praises?

Her Legacy of Prayer

For wisdom is more precious than rubies, and nothing you desire can compare with her.

—*Proverbs 8:11*

REFLECT ON: Proverbs 8:11–36.

PRAISE GOD: For the gift of wisdom, which preserves, blesses, and even prolongs our life.

OFFER THANKS: For the benefits of wisdom you have already
                 tasted in your daily life.

CONFESS: Any tendency to choose the wisdom of the
                 world over the wisdom of God.

ASK GOD: Every day to make you a woman who longs
                 for wisdom, who prefers it to silver and gold.

Lift Your Heart

*P*roverbs is full of pithy statements that contain profound wisdom
for daily life. Look through this book of Scripture and select a few
favorites, then commit them to memory. Here's a few to get you
started:

> *A cheerful heart is good medicine, but a crushed spirit dries up the bones.*
> *—Proverbs 17:22*

> *A fool finds no pleasure in understanding but delights in airing his*
> *own opinions.*
> *—Proverbs 18:2*

> *[She] who gets wisdom loves [her] own soul; [she] who cherishes*
> *understanding prospers.*
> *—Proverbs 19:8*

Lord, you know better than I the kind of heart in which wisdom grows
best—one in which patience, faith, and humility are there to nourish
it. Help me cultivate a heart in which wisdom can quickly take root
and flourish. Let wisdom be so much a part of my life that it produces
a shelter for others.

34

THE SHULAMMITE WOMAN

HER CHARACTER:	Hers is the only female voice that speaks directly to us in the Scripture. (Ruth's and Esther's voices, for instance, are mediated by narrators.) The Shulammite woman boldly declares her longing and desire to be united to her lover in marriage.
HER SORROW:	To have been separated from her beloved at times.
HER JOY:	To enjoy so passionate a love.
KEY SCRIPTURE:	Song of Songs 1–8

She was young, beautiful, and desirable. He was handsome, strong, and agile, a shepherd or a king who lavished strange praise upon his beloved. He compared her hair to a flock of goats running down a mountain slope; her nose to the tower of Lebanon, and her teeth ("each with its twin"!) to sheep that have just bathed. We smile in amusement at such images, understanding, however, that the Shulammite woman would have found them flattering. But we are more fascinated than amused by this beautifully written collection of love songs. And though we know it is not merely some ancient Valentine's Day card, we are not quite certain what to make of it.

Unlike any other book in the Bible, the Song of Songs is full of erotic imagery. The Shulammite woman was as passionate as her lover, initiating contact with him, openly declaring her feelings. She yearned for kisses from his mouth, so in love that even his name smelled sweet to her. She wandered the city at night (or dreamt of wandering it) searching for him. She wished she could pass him off as her brother so that she could kiss him publicly without creating a scandal. Each declaration from her elicited a passionate response from her lover, who sang of her,

> Your stature is like that of the palm,
>   and your breasts like clusters of fruit.
> I said, "I will climb the palm tree;
>   I will take hold of its fruit."
> May your breasts be like the clusters of the vine,
>   the fragrance of your breath like apples,
>   and your mouth like the best wine.
> —SONG OF SONGS 7:7–9

Despite the ancient imagery, we get the message.

The story of the Shulammite woman and her lover isn't properly a story, one with a clear narrative line, but a poetic expression of love in all its emotional variety and intensity. The songs capture the desire, the anguish, the tension, and the ecstasy of love. Speakers and scenes shift so quickly, however, that it can be difficult to tell who is speaking and what is going on. No wonder there have been so many different interpretations of the Song of Songs, more than any other book of the Old Testament.

What makes this portion of Scripture even more enigmatic is that it never once mentions God. But if God has nothing to do with these love songs, how did this material ever make it into the canon of Scripture in the first place?

The Jews believed the book was not primarily about individual lovers but about God's love for his people Israel. Christians initially read it as a parable of Christ's love for the church and later as a parable of his love for the individual soul. Modern commentators tend to view it more literally, as an expression of the sacredness of married life, the fullest expression of love between a man and a woman. They praise its inclusion in the Bible because it celebrates marital love and the sexual expression of that love. Anyone inclined to believe the Bible teaches a negative view of sex should read this book of Scripture before drawing such a conclusion.

But who wrote these eloquent love songs? Some say various poets, while others say they were written by Solomon in praise of one of his many wives. And yet others have suggested they were written by a woman. Whatever the case, most admit that the poetry of the Song of Songs can be understood in more than one way. The story of the Shulammite, mysterious as it is, touches our longing to love and be loved.

Her Legacy of Prayer

Place me like a seal over your heart,
    like a seal on your arm;
for love is as strong as death,
    its jealousy unyielding as the grave.
It burns like blazing fire,
    like a mighty flame.
Many waters cannot quench love;
    rivers cannot wash it away.
If one were to give
    all the wealth of his house for love,
    it would be utterly scorned.

                                   —Song of Songs 8:6–8

REFLECT ON: Songs of Songs 1:2–4; 2:10–13; 8:6–8.

PRAISE GOD: That nothing can separate us from his love.

OFFER THANKS: That Christ's passion has rendered us beautiful in the eyes of God.

CONFESS: Any failure to believe God truly is the Lover
                            of your soul.

ASK GOD: To help you enter into this dialogue of love
                            with him.

Lift Your Heart

The Shulammite woman was so captivated by her lover that his name
was like perfume that made everything in her world smell good. In biblical times, names actually revealed the person. Knowing someone's
name was equivalent to knowing that person's essence. This week, light
a fragrant candle as you take time to reflect on one or more of God's
names. Look up relevant Scripture passages and ask God to reveal himself more deeply to you.

Creator of Heaven and Earth (Genesis 14:19)

My Song (Exodus 15:2)

Prince of Peace (Isaiah 9:6)

Good Shepherd (John 10:14)

Counselor (John 14:26)

Father of Compassion (2 Corinthians 1:3)

Savior (1 Timothy 4:10)

Light (1 John 1:5)

---

*Lord, I have placed you as a seal over my heart. Neither death nor life,
neither angels nor demons, neither the present nor the future, nor any
powers, neither height nor depth, nor anything else in all creation, will
be able to separate me from your love.*

35

GOMER

Her Name Means
"Completion"

HER CHARACTER:	Though a married woman, she carried on numerous love affairs, crediting her lovers for the gifts her husband had given her.
HER SORROW:	To have become the symbol of spiritual adultery—a picture of Israel's unfaithfulness to God.
HER JOY:	That her husband continued to love her despite her unfaithfulness.
KEY SCRIPTURE:	Hosea 1–3

The man stood at the door, craning his neck and peering through the half-light. His limbs felt stiff and cold, despite the desert heat that still warmed the narrow street. Other than a stray dog curled in a knot against the wall of a neighboring house, he saw nothing. It was too late for a woman to be walking the streets alone. But, then, she wouldn't be alone, would she?

He didn't want to go inside yet, to listen to the absence of her chatter, to lie down on the empty bed. By noon tomorrow, the news of her betrayal would fill every gossip-hungry soul in town like swill in a pig's belly. Hosea, the man who would steer the nation with his prophecies, couldn't even control his own wife.

He felt grief and fury like a storm breaking inside him. He had meant to guard his heart; he had never intended to give himself so completely. His pain was the worse for loving her so well. For Gomer had squandered his gifts, mocked his tenderness, and allowed herself to be seduced by other lovers.

Hadn't God warned him and instructed him to "Go, take to yourself an adulterous wife and children of unfaithfulness, because the land is guilty of the vilest adultery in departing from the Lord"? He had named his children Jezreel ("God Scatters"), Lo-Ruhamah ("No Pity"), and Lo-Ammi ("Not My People"). Each successive child measured the growing rift between husband and wife. Hosea wondered whether he had even fathered the last two.

The word of the Lord that had filled Hosea's mouth now troubled his soul, rushing back with appalling force. So this was how God felt about his own people—bitterly betrayed, cut to the heart, disgusted, outraged. His tender love, his every gift meant nothing to a people enamored with Canaanite gods. Israel's leading men were the worst whores of all—virtuosos when it came to playing the harlot, cheating the poor, and imploring idols to bless them with peace and riches. But peace was elusive. Six kings had ruled the northern kingdom during a period of just twenty-five years. Four were murdered by their successors and one was captured in battle. All the while, Assyria perched like a vulture at its borders.

If only Israel would learn its lesson and turn back to the Lord before it was too late—if only Gomer would turn back. Hosea wanted to shout in her face, shake her awake to her sin. Enough of patience. Enough of tenderness. She had ignored his threats, shrugging them off as so many flies on a donkey. What choice had he now? He would find a way to punish her unfaithfulness.

In the midst of his bitter grief, he heard the voice of God, strong and clear: "Go, show your love to your wife again, though she is loved by another and is an adulteress. Love her as the Lord loves the Israelites, though they turn to other gods."

So Hosea took back the wife he couldn't stop loving. And the word of the Lord transformed Lo-Ruhamah into Ruhamah ("Loved") and Lo-Ammi into Ammi ("My People").

The story of Gomer and Hosea portrays God's jealousy for his people. For the first time, a prophet dared to speak of God as a husband and Israel as his bride. But this is a tangled love story, one in which God's heart is repeatedly broken. Despite his pleas, regardless of his threats, Israel would not turn back to him until after the northern kingdom was destroyed by Assyria a few years later. Still, the knit-together lives of Hosea and Gomer were a living reminder to the Israelites of both God's judgment and his love. Hosea's beautiful words still move us as we think about the church today, about our own unfaithfulness and God's forgiveness: "I will betroth you to me forever; I will betroth you in righteousness and justice, in love and compassion. Let us acknowledge the Lord; let us press on to acknowledge him. As surely as the sun rises, he will appear; he will come to us like the winter rains, like the spring rains that water the earth."

No longer Lo-Ruhamah, we are Ruhamah ("Loved"), and no longer Lo-Ammi but Ammi ("My People"). For our Maker has become our Husband, the one who punishes our sin but loves us still.

Her Legacy of Prayer

"In that day," declares the LORD, "you will call me 'my husband'; you will no longer call me 'my master.'"

—*Hosea 2:16*

REFLECT ON: Hosea 1–3.

PRAISE GOD: For his mercy.

OFFER THANKS: That God loved you before you ever thought of loving him.

CONFESS: Any tendency to love money, pleasure, children,
                      husband, or career more than you love God.

ASK GOD: To increase your hunger to know him more
                      intimately.

Lift Your Heart

Sometimes couples grow apart not because either have been unfaith-
ful, but because of sheer busyness. If your relationship with God is bog-
ging down in life's details, why not plan an intimate evening or
weekend with him? Let it be a time of quieting your soul in his presence, of hushing life's everyday demands. Spend the day walking a soli-
tary beach, or hidden away at a retreat center or a friend's cottage or
cabin. Take your Bible and a book of poetry by Christina Rossetti or
Ken Gire's *Intimate Moments with the Savior* or C. S. Lewis's *The Lion,
the Witch and the Wardrobe* or Kathleen Norris's *The Cloister Walk*. If
you're artistic, bring paint and art paper and commune with God
through the pictures you create. Let it be a time of praising God, of
telling him how much you love him, of thanking him for all the ways
he has loved you. Don't try to have a great spiritual experience; just
relax and let God know you want to be with him.

---

*Lord, how can I begin to understand how faithfully you've loved me?
Draw me into your presence and hold me close. Quiet my noisy heart
and speak to me.*

36

ELIZABETH

Her Name Means
"God Is My Oath"

HER CHARACTER:	A descendant of Aaron, Elizabeth was a woman the Bible calls "upright in the sight of God." Like very few others, male or female, she is praised for observing all the Lord's commandments and regulations without blame. She is the first to acknowledge Jesus as Lord.
HER SORROW:	To be barren for most of her life.
HER JOY:	To give birth to John, later known as John the Baptist, the Messiah's forerunner. His name, divinely assigned, meant "the Lord is gracious."
KEY SCRIPTURE:	Luke 1:5–80

꒡

er eyes were a golden brown. Like currants set in pastry, they winked out at the world from cheeks that had baked too long in the sun. Snowy strands of hair straggled from beneath a woolen shawl, tickling her wrinkled face. Small hands rested tenderly on her rounded belly, softly probing for any hint of movement. But all was still. From her vantage point on the roof of the house, she noticed a figure walking up the pathway and wondered who her visitor might be.

She and Zechariah had been content enough in their quiet house these last few months, secluded in their joy. Each morning she had opened her eyes as though waking to a fantastic dream. Sometimes she shook with laughter as she thought about how God had rearranged her life, planting a child in her shriveled up, old-woman's womb.

Six months ago, Zechariah had been chosen by lot to burn incense before the Most Holy Place, a once-in-a-lifetime privilege. But during his week of priestly service in the temple, he had been frightened half to death by a figure that appeared suddenly next to the altar of incense. "Your wife Elizabeth will bear you a son," the angel told him, "and you are to give him the name John. He will be a joy and delight to you, and many will rejoice because of his birth, for he will be great in the sight of the Lord." It was Sarah and Abraham all over, Rebekah and Isaac, Rachel and Jacob. God was once again kindling a fire with two dry sticks.

For the life of her, Elizabeth couldn't understand her husband's response to the angel that had so terrified him. Once you'd laid eyes on a heavenly being, how could you fail to believe that anything was possible? But Zechariah had blurted out his skepticism and suffered the consequences. His voice had been snatched away and would not be given back until the angel's words came to pass. These days he communicated by scribbling on a wax tablet.

Elizabeth looked down again at the figure advancing up the path, a green sprig of a girl. The older woman stepped carefully down the stairs and into the house to welcome her guest. But with the young woman's words of greeting came something that felt like a gale-force wind, shaking the beams and rafters of the house. Steadying herself, the older woman felt suddenly invigorated. Her unborn baby leapt inside her as she shouted out a welcoming response:

"Blessed are you among women, and blessed is the child you will bear! But why am I so favored, that the mother of my Lord should come to me? As soon as the sound of your greeting reached my ears, the baby in my womb leaped for joy. Blessed is she who has believed that what the Lord has said to her will be accomplished!"

Mary had made the journey all the way from Nazareth to visit her relative, Elizabeth. The same angel who had spoken to Zechariah in the temple had whispered the secret of the older woman's pregnancy to the virgin, who was also with child. The magnificent song of praise that burst from Mary's lips during their meeting may have taken shape during the course of her sixty-mile journey south, to the hill country of Judea where Elizabeth lived:

My soul glorifies the Lord
    and my spirit rejoices in God my Savior,
for he has been mindful
    of the humble state of his servant.
From now on all generations will call me blessed,
    for the Mighty One has done great things for me—
    holy is his name.
His mercy extends to those who fear him,
    from generation to generation.
He has performed mighty deeds with his arm;
    he has scattered those who are proud in their inmost thoughts.
He has brought down rulers from their thrones
    but has lifted up the humble.
He has filled the hungry with good things
    but has sent the rich away empty.
He has helped his servant Israel,
    remembering to be merciful
to Abraham and his descendants forever,
    even as he said to our fathers.

The two women held each other, their bonds of kinship now so much stronger than what mere flesh and blood could forge. For Israel's God—the God of Sarah, Rebekah, Rachel, Leah, Miriam, Deborah, Naomi, Ruth, Abigail, and Hannah—was on the move again, bringing the long-ago promise to fulfillment. And blessed was she who did not doubt that what the Lord had said to her would be accomplished.

Her Legacy of Prayer

*"Blessed is she who has believed that what the Lord has said to her
will be accomplished!"*

—*Luke 1:45*

REFLECT ON: Luke 1:5–80.

PRAISE GOD: That he is the Creator who shapes every child
                   in the womb.

OFFER THANKS: For the gift of children.

CONFESS: Any tendency to cheapen the value of human
                   life, including unborn life.

ASK GOD: To restore our appreciation for the miracle of
                   human life.

Lift Your Heart

A person's a person, no matter how small!
—*From* Horton Hears a Who *by Dr. Seuss*

Mary's visit to Elizabeth probably occurred when Elizabeth was in
her sixth month of pregnancy. The younger woman may have stayed
long enough to help the older one with her delivery. In any case, Mary
would have been in the first trimester of her pregnancy and Elizabeth
in her third. Here's what would have been happening to the children
growing in their wombs:

Jesus:

        18 days—his nervous system appeared.
        30 days—most of his major organ systems had begun to form.

4 weeks—his heart began beating.
7 weeks—his facial features would have been visible.
8 weeks—all his major body structures and organs were present.
10 weeks—tiny teeth were forming in his gums.
12 weeks—his brain was fully formed and he could feel pain.
He may have even sucked his thumb.

John:

6th month—he could grasp his hands, kick, do somersaults,
and hear voices and sounds outside the womb.

Take a few moments to praise your Creator with beautiful words
from Psalm 139:

For you created my inmost being;
your knit me together in my mother's womb.
I praise you because I am fearfully and wonderfully made;
your works are wonderful,
I know that full well.
My frame was not hidden from you
when I was made in the secret place.
When I was woven together in the depths of the earth,
your eyes saw my unformed body.
All the days ordained for me
were written in your book
before one of them came to be.

You are the Lord and Giver of life. Help me to respect, protect, and
nurture it—no matter what color, no matter what age, no matter what
gender of human being I encounter.

37

MARY, THE MOTHER OF JESUS

Her Name May Mean "Bitterness"

HER CHARACTER:	She was a virgin from a poor family in an obscure village in Galilee. Her response to Gabriel reveals a young woman of unusual faith and humility. Her unqualified yes to God's plan for her life entailed great personal risk and suffering. She must have endured seasons of confusion, fear, and darkness as the events of her life unfolded. She is honored, not only as the mother of Jesus, but as his first disciple.
HER SORROW:	To see the son she loved shamed and tortured, left to die like the worst kind of criminal.
HER JOY:	To see her child raised from the dead; to have received the Holy Spirit along with Jesus' other disciples.
KEY SCRIPTURES:	Matthew 1:18–25; 2; Luke 1:26–80; 2; John 19:25–27

She sat down on the bench and closed her eyes, an old woman silhouetted against the blue Jerusalem sky. Even the wood beneath her conjured images. Though she could no longer recall the exact curl of his smile or the shape of his sleeping face resting next to hers, she could

still see the rough brown hands, expertly molding the wood to his purposes. Joseph had been a good carpenter and an even better husband.

These days the memories came unbidden, like a gusty wind carrying her away to other times and places. Some said drowning men see
their lives unfold in incredible detail just before they die. Age had a similar effect, she thought, except that you could relive your memories
with a great deal more leisure. . . .

A cool breeze teased at her skirts as she balanced the jug on her head,
making her way toward the well. A stranger, she noticed, was approaching from the opposite direction. Even in the dusky light, his clothes
shone, as though bleached bright by the strongest of soap.

"Greetings," he shouted, "you who are highly favored! The Lord
is with you."

No Nazarene, she was sure, would ever dare greet a maiden like
that. But with each step his words grew bolder, not softer, rushing
toward her like water plunging over a cliff:

"Do not be afraid, Mary. . . .
  you have found favor with God. . . .
  you will give birth to a son. . . .
    He will be called the Son of the Most High. . . .
    the Holy Spirit will come upon you. . . .
      Elizabeth your relative is going to have a child in her old age."

Wave after wave broke over her as she listened to the angel's
words—first confusion and fear, then awe and gratitude, and finally a
rush of joy and peace. Her whole being was drenched in light. Then
she heard more words, this time cascading from her lips, not his:

"I am the Lord's servant.
  May it be to me as you have said."

Though the angel departed, Mary's peace remained. The Most
High had visited the lowliest of his servants and spoken the promise

every Jewish woman longed to hear: "You will be with child and give birth to a son, and you are to give him the name Jesus. The Lord God will give him the throne of his father David, and he will reign over the house of Jacob forever; his kingdom will never end."

The moon hung like a smile in the night sky as she lifted the brimming jug and began walking across the fields. As the water swayed and splashed to the rhythm of her movements, she realized that she, too, felt full and satisfied—as though she had just finished a favorite meal. Questions, she knew, would come with the morning. For now, it was enough to look up at the stars and know that God was at work shaping her future.

"Mama, Mama," he yelled, running toward her, chubby arms flung out beseechingly.

"Jesus, what is it now, child?" she smiled, scooping the chunky boy into her arms before he could topple over in the usual tangle of arms and legs. But he was all kisses, squealing and nuzzling his curly head against her breast, as though to bury himself in her soft, warm flesh. She sighed contentedly. How many mothers had she known? But none had adequately described the sheer wonder of a child—the laughter, the constant surprise, the tenderness. Not to mention the fear and worry that were also part of it.

But this was no time to entertain such thoughts. The men from the East had recently left. How strange these Magi seemed, with their tales of a star that had led them all the way to Bethlehem in search of a new king. They had bowed before her dark-eyed child, laying out their treasures of gold, incense, and myrrh—as though paying homage to royalty. One morning, however, they had packed in haste, saying only that a dream had warned them to return home without reporting news of their successful search to the king. Even the mention of Herod's name had filled her with dread. Bethlehem lay just six miles south of Jerusalem—dangerously close to a man who had murdered his own children out of jealousy for his throne. How would such a ruler respond to rumors of a child-king in Bethlehem?

Two nights ago Joseph had shaken her awake, shushing her with details of the dream he had just had. "Mary, an angel appeared to me. We must leave before sunrise. Herod plans to search for our child and kill him!"

Now they were on their way to Egypt, reversing the steps of Moses, Aaron, and Miriam, who had led her ancestors to freedom so long ago. Mary wondered, as they rested, if they would ever see their homeland again.

"Woman," Jesus breathed the word softly. His lean arms were flung out on either side of him, as though imploringly. The palms of his hands were pinned with spikes. He looked at her first and then at the young man standing beside her. "Here is your son." The words came haltingly.

Then to the man, he sighed: "Here is your mother."

She wanted to reach for him with all the might of her love, to bury his sorrow in her breasts, to tell him he was the son she needed most. Would not the God who pitied Abraham also pity her? Would he allow her to suffer what even the patriarch had been spared—the sacrifice of a child? All her life she had loved the God whose angel had spoken to her, calling her "highly favored." But how could a woman whose son was dying on a Roman cross ever consider herself "favored"?

Suddenly her own words came back to her, as though a younger version of herself was whispering them in her ear: "I am the Lord's servant. May it be to me as you have said."

The midday sky had blackened, but she could still see her son's twisted form on the cross, his eyes searching hers. Thorns circled his forehead in the shape of a crown, a crude reminder of the sign the Roman governor had fastened to the wood: "Jesus of Nazareth, King of the Jews."

She thought of the Magi and their priceless gifts. The gold and incense, royal treasures that had helped them survive their stay in Egypt. She had always wondered about the myrrh. Now she knew—it was embalming oil for the king the wise men had come to worship.

"My God, my God, why have you forsaken me?" The cry pierced her like a sword driven through her chest. The earth shook violently and she fell to her knees, barely able to complete the words of the psalm for the man who hung dead on the cross:

> O my God, I cry out by day, but you do not answer,
>> by night, and am not silent. . . .
> But I am a worm and not a man,
>> scorned by men and despised by the people.
> All who see me mock me;
>> they hurl insults, shaking their heads. . . .
> Yet you brought me out of the womb;
>> you made me trust in you
>> even at my mother's breast.
> From birth I was cast upon you;
>> from my mother's womb you have been my God. . . .
>> they have pierced my hands and my feet.
> I can count all my bones;
>> people stare and gloat over me,
> They divide my garments among them
>> and cast lots for my clothing.
> But you, O Lord, be not far off;
>> O my Strength, come quickly to help me. . . .
> You who fear the Lord, praise him!
>> All you descendants of Jacob, honor him! . . .
>> future generations will be told about the Lord.
> They will proclaim his righteousness
>> to a people yet unborn—
>> for he has done it.
>
> —PSALM 22

By the time Mary opened her eyes, the setting sun had turned the city into a golden land. She smiled, wiping the tears from her wrinkled face. How true the angel's words had been. No woman from Eve onward had ever been blessed as she, the mother of the Messiah, had been. Yes, the past was alive inside her, but it was the future that filled her with joy. Soon, she would see her son again, and this time it would be his hands that would wipe away the last of her tears.

Her Legacy of Prayer

"Greetings, you who are highly favored! The Lord is with you."
—Luke 1:28

REFLECT ON:	Luke 1:26–38.
PRAISE GOD:	That nothing is impossible with him.
OFFER THANKS:	That a woman's body became the dwelling place of divinity.
CONFESS:	Any tendency to devalue yourself as a woman.
ASK GOD:	To make you a woman, like Mary, who brings Jesus into the world by expressing his character, power, forgiveness, and grace.

Lift Your Heart

Choose one episode in the life of Mary—her encounter with Gabriel, the birth of her child, the scene with the shepherds, the presentation in the temple, the Magi's visit, the escape to Egypt, her son's agony on the cross, or her presence with the disciples in the Upper Room. Imagine yourself in her place. What are your struggles, your joys? What thoughts run through your mind? Does anything or anyone take you by surprise? Ask the Holy Spirit to guide your reflections, to help you imagine the sounds, sights, and smells that will bring each scene to life. Let the Scriptures feed your soul with a deeper understanding of God's intention for your life. Pray for the grace to be like the woman who said: "I am the Lord's servant. May it be to me as you have said."

———————

My soul is full of you, my God, and I cannot hold back my gladness. Everyone who sees me will call me blessed because you have noticed me. You saw my lowliness and my need and filled my emptiness with your presence. Form your likeness in me so that, like Mary, I can bring you into a world that desperately needs your love.

38

ANNA

Her Name Means
"Favor" or "Grace"

———————

HER CHARACTER:	Married for only seven years, she spent the long years of her widowhood fasting and praying in the temple, abandoning herself entirely to God. A prophetess, she was one of the first to bear witness to Jesus.
HER SORROW:	As a widow, she would probably have been among the most vulnerable members of society, with no one to provide for her financially or to take care of her if her health failed.
HER JOY:	That her own eyes beheld the Messiah she had longed to see.
KEY SCRIPTURE:	Luke 2:22–38

———————

A small bird darted past the Court of the Gentiles, flew up to the Women's Court, and then on to the Court of Israel—one of the inner courts of the temple, accessible only to men. Anna blinked as she watched the beating wings swerve into the sunlight and vanish. She wondered into which privileged corner the little bird had disappeared.

For most of her eighty-four years, she had been a widow who spent her days praying and fasting in the temple. Though Anna had walked past the outer court thousands of times, she never failed to notice the warning inscribed in its walls in both Greek and Latin: "No stranger is to enter within the balustrade round the temple and enclosure. Whoever is caught will be responsible to himself for his death, which will ensue." It was an awesome thing to come into the Presence of the Holy One.

Though she could not echo the prayer of Jewish men, who praised God for creating them neither Gentiles nor women, she could at least be grateful for the privilege of ascending beyond the Court of the Gentiles to the Women's Court, where she would be that much closer to the Most Holy Place. Having done so, she bowed her head, rocking back and forth to the rhythm of her prayers:

> *How lovely is your dwelling place,*
> *O Lord Almighty!*
> *My soul yearns, even faints,*
> *for the courts of the Lord;*
> *my heart and my flesh cry out*
> *for the living God.*
> *Even the sparrow has found a home,*
> *and the swallow a nest for herself,*
> *where she may have her young—*
> *a place near your altar,*
> *O Lord Almighty, my King and my God.*

—PSALM 84:1–3

Suddenly a voice interrupted her recitation of the familiar psalm. Old Simeon, she saw, was holding a baby to his breast, shouting out words that thrilled her soul. "Sovereign Lord, as you have promised, you now dismiss your servant in peace. For my eyes have seen your salvation, which you have prepared in the sight of all people, a light for revelation to the Gentiles and for glory to your people Israel."

Like her, Simeon had lived for nothing but Israel's consolation—though he had not seen, yet he had believed. Anna watched as the child's parents hung on the old man's words. Then he handed the infant back to his mother, this time speaking more softly. "This child is destined to cause the falling and rising of many in Israel, and to be a sign that will be spoken against, so that the thoughts of many hearts will be revealed. And a sword will pierce your own soul too."

Anna placed her arms gently around the young mother's shoulders and gazed at the sleeping infant. Words of thanksgiving spilled from her lips. Her heart felt buoyant, her hope unsinkable. More vividly than Jacob, who had dreamed of a ladder full of angels, or Moses, who had beheld a bush burning in the desert, she, Anna, a widow and prophetess from the tribe of Asher, had just experienced the very presence of God. Her eyes had seen the promised child, whose brilliance would scatter the darkness and bring deliverance for all God's people.

Now she, too, felt like a sparrow soaring freely in the house of God. It no longer mattered that she was forbidden entry into the innermost courts of the temple. God himself was breaking down the dividing walls between Jew and Gentile, male and female, revealing himself to all who hungered for his presence. That day a child had transformed the Women's Court into the holiest place of all.

Scripture doesn't tell us whether Anna ever actually wished she were allowed to enter the innermost courts of the temple in Jerusalem. But her longing for God is obvious. Clearly, she was a woman with a great spiritual appetite, who abandoned her life to God and was rewarded by meeting Jesus and his parents just forty days after his birth, during the presentation in the temple.

Her Legacy of Prayer

She never left the temple but worshiped night and day, fasting and praying.

—*Luke 2:37*

REFLECT ON: Luke 2:36–38.

PRAISE GOD: That Jesus is the true Bread from heaven, who satisfies the hungry heart.

OFFER THANKS: For men and women who hunger and thirst for God's kingdom.

CONFESS: Any tendency to be so locked into your own
                        concerns that you fail to pray for others in
                        need.

ASK GOD: To increase your hunger for his kingdom.

Lift Your Heart

Anna did more than merely long for the coming Messiah; she prayed and fasted daily for the coming of God's kingdom. Even though Christianity has spread across the globe, there are still many people who suffer from war and injustice, many who have little or nothing to eat, and many more who live in spiritual darkness. This week stretch yourself beyond your immediate concerns. Look at an atlas, a map, or a globe, and choose a country for which to pray. Read newspaper reports and magazine articles that will help you understand what is going on in that nation. Fast and pray for peace, for daily bread, for freedom, for justice, and for Christ's light to shine upon that people.

Jesus, I long for your light to spread across the whole earth so that peoples from every land will know you. Today, give me a burden for another nation or ethnic group that knows little of you. Show me how to pray in a way that builds your kingdom.

39

THE WOMAN
OF SAMARIA

HER CHARACTER:	Looked down upon by the Jews because she was a Samaritan, and disdained because of her many romantic liaisons, she would not have been most people's first choice to advance the gospel in a region where it had not yet been heard.
HER SORROW:	To have lived in a way that relegated her to the margins of her society.
HER JOY:	That Jesus broke through barriers of culture, race, and religion in order to reveal himself to her.
KEY SCRIPTURE:	John 4:1–42

Every day, the woman carried her water jug to Jacob's well just outside Sychar, a town midway between Jerusalem and Nazareth. Even though it was the hottest time of the day, she preferred it to the evening hours, when the other women gathered. How tired she was of their wagging tongues. Better the scorching heat than their sharp remarks.

She was surprised, however, to see that today someone had already arrived at the well—a Jew from Galilee by the look of him. At least she had nothing to fear from his tongue, for Jews did their best to avoid Samaritans, despising them as half-breeds who worshiped not in the temple at Jerusalem but at their shrine on Mount Gerizim. For once she was glad to be ignored, grateful that men did not address women in public.

But as she approached the well, the man startled her, breaking the rules she had counted on to protect her. "Will you give me a drink?" he asked.

What kind of a Jew was this? she wondered. Certainly not a Pharisee, or he would have taken the long way around Samaria to get to Galilee. With a toss of her head, she replied, "You are a Jew and I am a Samaritan woman. How can you ask me for a drink?"

But he wouldn't be put off. "If you knew the gift of God and who it is that asks you for a drink, you would have asked him and he would have given you living water."

"Sir," she replied, "you have nothing to draw with and the well is deep. Where can you get this living water? Are you greater than our father Jacob, who gave us the well and drank from it himself, as did also his sons and his flocks and herds?" That should take him down a notch or two.

But the man kept pressing. "Go," he told her, "call your husband and come back."

This last request took the wind out of her. Her quick tongue was barely able to reply, "I have no husband."

"You are right when you say you have no husband," Jesus said. "The fact is, you have had five husbands, and the man you now have is not your husband. What you have just said is quite true."

His words cut her. Shaking off the hurt, she tried changing the subject, diverting him by stirring up the old controversy between Jews and Samaritans, asking, "Sir, I can see that you are a prophet. Our fathers worshiped on this mountain, but you Jews claim that the place where we must worship is in Jerusalem."

Jesus declared, "Believe me, woman, a time is coming when you will worship the Father neither on this mountain nor in Jerusalem. You Samaritans worship what you do not know; we worship what we do know, for salvation is from the Jews. Yet a time is coming and has now come when the true worshipers will worship the Father in spirit and truth, for they are the kind of worshipers the Father seeks."

The woman said, "I know that Messiah is coming. When he comes, he will explain everything to us."

Then Jesus declared, "I who speak to you am he."

Leaving her water jar, the woman went back to the town and said to the people, "Come see a man who told me everything I ever did. Could this be the Christ?"

Meanwhile, his disciples, who had gone into the town to look for food, returned and urged him, "Rabbi, eat something."

But Jesus replied, "I have food to eat that you know nothing about."

Dodge, counterdodge—nothing the woman said would keep Jesus at bay. He kept pressing beneath the surface, inviting her to a deeper understanding, hemming her in by revealing his knowledge of the most intimate details of her life. Overwhelmed, she finally admitted the truth. And when she did, Jesus startled her with a revelation about himself: he admitted, for the first time, that he was the Messiah. Though she hadn't known it, she had been conversing with her Savior.

Jesus had arrived at the well thirsty, hungry, and tired from the journey north to Galilee. But by the time his disciples returned from their shopping trip in Sychar, he seemed refreshed and restored by his encounter with the woman.

She, in turn, was so deeply affected by him that she exclaimed to whoever would listen: "He told me everything I ever did." At the Samaritans' urging, Jesus stayed on for two days and many came to believe, saying to the woman: "We no longer believe just because of what you said; now we have heard for ourselves and we know that this man really is the Savior of the world."

Her Legacy of Prayer

Then, leaving her water jar, the woman went back to the town and said to the people, "Come, see a man who told me everything I ever

*did. Could this be the Christ?" They came out of the town and made
their way toward him.*

—John 4:28–30

REFLECT ON: John 4:4–42.

PRAISE GOD: Because in his kingdom, the last shall be first.

OFFER THANKS: For the way he has uncovered your need for
                   him.

CONFESS: Any tendency to act as though God cannot
                   use your neediness but only your strength.

ASK GOD: To give you the humility to face the depth of
                   your need for grace.

Lift Your Heart

It's always difficult to admit our sins, particularly if we think God will
love us only if we behave well. Though we might never articulate such
a thought, it shapes our theology more than we like to admit. This
week, make a list of everything God knows about you that you wish
he didn't. Thank him for loving you despite your sins. Then tear up the
list, remembering the words of Psalm 103: "For as high as the heavens
are above the earth, so great is his love for those who fear him; as far
as the east is from the west, so far has he removed our transgressions
from us."

————————————

*Lord, you know everything about me, even the things I'm hiding from
myself. Give me the grace to admit my sin, believing that though you see
me, you still love me. Help me to let go of anything that keeps me from
experiencing the living water of your Holy Spirit welling up inside me.*

40

THE WOMAN WHO LIVED A SINFUL LIFE

HER CHARACTER: She was a notorious sinner, possibly a prostitute or adulteress. Rather than trying to defend what was indefensible in her life, she admitted her sin and made a spectacle of herself in a passionate display of love and gratitude.

HER SORROW: That she had offended God so grievously.

HER JOY: That Jesus forgave her sins and commended her for her great faith and love.

KEY SCRIPTURE: Luke 7:36–50

$\nearrow$

The woman felt as though her world had unraveled in a moment's time. Doors had opened, walls had crumbled, thoughts of her future no longer frightened but thrilled her. She felt clean and whole, innocent as a girl still living in her father's house. Her heart was a wild confusion of sorrow and joy as she followed the rabbi through the doorway.

Ignoring the stares of the men, she walked over to the place where Jesus was reclining at a table. In her hands she held an alabaster jar of perfume. Her body trembled as she approached. She hardly knew what she was doing as she covered his feet with her kisses and then anointed them with the precious perfume, wiping his feet with her hair. How else could she express her heart to the man who had loved her so well?

Like any good Pharisee, Simon loved the law, measuring his days by the steady rhythm of the regulations by which he lived. They were a fence safeguarding his purity, protecting his sense of settled security. How good of the holy God to provide a map for the righteous, a way of life to set him apart from ordinary Jews—like the woman who had just walked through the door, hoping to glean a few scraps from his table.

Simon was surprised that a sinful woman, even a hungry one, would enter his house. But his surprise grew as he noticed she was not eating but weeping so profusely that her tears were spilling onto the feet of one of his guests. Everything about the scene repelled him and offended his sense of order—a notorious harlot kissing the man's feet, wiping them with her hair, and then pouring perfume over them. It was an astonishing performance.

Even more astonishing was the fact that his guest seemed to enjoy the attention. "If this man were a prophet," Simon thought, "he would know who is touching him and what kind of woman she is—that she is a sinner." All of his questions about Jesus were put to rest by the scene he had just witnessed. His ordered way of looking at the world was safe enough, bolstered by the judgment he had rendered.

As though he had overheard Simon's secret thoughts, Jesus turned and spoke to him. "Simon, I have something to tell you.

"Two men owed money to a certain moneylender. One owed him five hundred denarii, and the other fifty. Neither of them had the money to pay him back, so he canceled the debts of both. Now which of them will love him more?"

Simon replied, "I suppose the one who had the bigger debt canceled."

"You have judged correctly," Jesus said.

Then he turned toward the woman and said to Simon, "Do you see this woman? I came into your house. You did not give me any water for my feet, but she wet my feet with her tears and wiped them with her hair. You did not give me a kiss, but this woman, from the time I entered, has not stopped kissing my feet. You did not put oil on my head, but she has poured perfume on my feet. Therefore, I tell you, her many sins have been forgiven—for she loved much. But he who has been forgiven little loves little."

The other guests began to say among themselves, "Who is this who even forgives sins?"

Jesus said to the woman, "Your faith has saved you; go in peace."

Though this woman was a notorious sinner, she recognized her great need for grace. Repentance turned her world on its head, opening up an entirely new view of things. Simon, by contrast, was a religious man who, no doubt, had done his best to live a respectable life. His sin was tucked away, hidden even from himself. His habit of judging others had formed a fence around his one-dimensional view of the universe, shielding his neat and orderly life from the unpredictable power of grace.

But Simon and the woman both owed a debt they could not possibly repay. Though Simon's sin was less obvious, it was the more dangerous. He was like a man who was following a map he was certain would lead to heaven—but when heaven came down and walked into his house, he didn't even know it. The woman, on the other hand, realized just how lost she had been. Forgiven much, she loved much. She found heaven at the feet of Jesus.

Her Legacy of Prayer

Therefore I tell you, her many sins have been forgiven—for she loved much. But he who has been forgiven little loves little.

—Luke 7:47

REFLECT ON: Luke 7:36–50.

PRAISE GOD: For the power of forgiveness in your own life.

OFFER THANKS: That God is still ready to forgive you, no matter how frequently or how seriously you have sinned.

CONFESS: Any self-righteousness that has crept into
                    your life.

ASK GOD: To protect you against pride, to enable you to
                    see your sins and believe in his desire and
                    power to forgive you.

Lift Your Heart

*H*ow long has it been since tears of repentance have washed your
soul? Do you find it easier to linger over others' failings than over
your own? Harsh attitudes toward the notorious sins of others—even
the sins of unprincipled politicians or insensitive husbands—will only
dry up your love for God.

No matter how long it's been since you committed your life to
God, pride has a way of creeping back in, locking you into a black-
and-white vision of the universe. Remember that the Pharisee was forgiven little, not because his sin was inconsequential but because his
repentance was so small. This week, search your heart for any judgments, large or small, you have made against others. Make a list of
people you feel have wronged you. Release your judgments against
them and ask God to bless them. Then tear up the sheet as a sign that
you are repenting of the judgments you made. The next time you are
tempted to judge someone, quickly repeat this exercise in your mind.

---

*Lord, when others rejected me, you embraced me. What was untouch-
able in me you touched. Make me a woman who loves much, a woman
who is not afraid to fall at your feet, bathing them with her tears.*

41

THE WOMAN WITH THE ISSUE OF BLOOD

HER CHARACTER:	So desperate for healing, she ignored the conventions of the day just for the chance to touch Jesus.
HER SORROW:	To have suffered a chronic illness that isolated her from others.
HER JOY:	That after long years of suffering, she finally found peace and freedom.
KEY SCRIPTURES:	Matthew 9:20–22; Mark 5:25–34; Luke 8:43–48

❧

*T*he woman hovered at the edge of the crowd. Nobody watched as she melted into the throng of bodies—just one more bee entering the hive. Her shame faded, quickly replaced by a rush of relief. No one had prevented her from joining in. No one had recoiled at her touch.

She pressed closer, but a noisy swarm of men still blocked her view. She could hear Jairus, a ruler of the synagogue, raising his voice above the others, pleading with Jesus to come and heal his daughter before it was too late.

Suddenly the group in front of her shifted, parting like the waters of the Jordan before the children of promise. It was all she needed. Her arm darted through the opening, fingers brushing the hem of his garment. Instantly, she felt a warmth spread through her, flushing out the pain, clearing out the decay. Her skin prickled and shivered. She felt strong and able, like a young girl coming into her own—so glad and giddy, in fact, that her feet wanted to rush her away before she created a spectacle by laughing out loud at her quiet miracle.

But Jesus blocked her escape and silenced the crowd with a curious question: "Who touched me?"

"Who touched him? He must be joking!" voices murmured. "People are pushing and shoving just to get near him!"

Shaking now, the woman fell at his feet. "For twelve years, I have been hemorrhaging and have spent all my money on doctors but have only grown worse. Today, I knew that if I could just touch your garment, I would be healed." But touching, she knew, meant spreading her defilement—even to the rabbi.

Twelve years of loneliness. Twelve years in which physicians had bled her of all her wealth. Her private affliction becoming a matter of public record. Every cup she handled, every chair she sat on could transmit defilement to others. Even though her impurity was considered a ritual matter rather than an ethical one, it had rendered her an outcast, making it impossible for her to live with a husband, bear a child, or enjoy the intimacy of friends and family. Surely the rabbi would censure her.

But instead of scolding and shaming her, Jesus praised her. "Daughter, your faith has healed you. Go in peace and be freed from your suffering."

His words must have been like water breaching a dam, breaking through her isolation, setting her free. He had addressed her not harshly, but tenderly, not as "woman" or "sinner," but rather as daughter. She was no longer alone, but part of his family by virtue of her faith.

That day, countless men and women had brushed against Jesus, but only one had truly touched him. And instead of being defiled by contact with her, his own touch had proven the more contagious, rendering her pure and whole again.

Her Legacy of Prayer

When she heard about Jesus, she came up behind him in the crowd and touched his cloak, because she thought, "If I just touch his clothes, I will be healed."

—Mark 5:27–28

REFLECT ON: Mark 5:21–34.

PRAISE GOD: That his touch produces peace and freedom.

OFFER THANKS: That faith is a gift that increases with use.

CONFESS: Any tendency to play it so safe you actually begin to suffocate the faith you have.

ASK GOD.   To bring this woman's story to mind the next time you are faced with an opportunity to exercise real faith.

Lift Your Heart

Trying to live the Christian life without faith is like trying to eat a steak with a straw, or kissing someone without using your lips, or propelling an airplane with foot pedals. It doesn't nourish you, never thrills you, and won't get you anywhere. If you feel the spark of faith fading, ask God to take the little you have and fan it to flame. Before you go to bed each night this week, remind yourself of your need by lighting a small candle at your bedside and pray this prayer:

Father, forgive my little faith
Make it big
Reduce my ego
Make it small
Give me a chance
To touch you and be touched
No matter how foolish
No matter how frightened
No matter how strange I feel
Fan my small spark into a brightness
Lighting the way ahead
Amen.

Pray it like you mean it, and God will not fail to provide you with opportunities to exercise your faith. (Don't forget to blow out the candle before you close your eyes!)

42

HERODIAS

Her Name, the Female Form
of "Herod," Means "Heroic"

HER CHARACTER:	A proud woman, she used her daughter to manipulate her husband into doing her will. She acted arrogantly, from beginning to end, in complete disregard for the laws of the land.
HER SHAME:	To be rebuked by an upstart prophet for leaving her husband, Philip, in order to marry his half brother Herod Antipas.
HER TRIUMPH:	That her scheme to murder her enemy, John the Baptist, worked.
KEY SCRIPTURES:	Matthew 14:3–12; Mark 6:14–29; Luke 3:19–20; 9:7–9

er grandfather, Herod the Great, had ruled Judea for thirty-four years. He had brought prosperity to a troubled region of the Roman Empire, building theaters, amphitheaters, and race courses, as well as a palace and a magnificent temple in Jerusalem. Despite such ambitious endeavors, he had even contrived to lower taxes on two occasions.

But Herod's reign contained shadows that darkened as the years went on. Herodias knew the stories well—how her grandfather had slaughtered a passel of Jewish brats in Bethlehem, how he had murdered his favorite wife (her own grandmother) and three of his sons for real or imagined intrigues. Advancing age and illness did nothing to improve his character. Herod was determined, in fact, that his own death would produce a time of universal mourning rather than celebration. So, in a final malevolent act, he commanded all the leading Jews to gather in Jericho. Then he imprisoned them in a stadium and ordered them to be executed at the moment of his death. But the king was cheated of his last wish: His prisoners had been set free as soon as he died in the spring of 4 B.C.

Not a nice man, her grandfather. But then, she thought, kings were a rather different order of human beings.

Herodias's husband and his half brother Antipas had been lucky survivors of Herod the Great's bloody family, but Antipas had proved the luckier of the two. For while Philip and Herodias languished in Rome with no one to rule, Antipas had been appointed tetrarch of Galilee and Perea. She could feel the man's power when he first visited them in Rome. And power was her favorite aphrodisiac.

Though Herod Antipas was married to the daughter of King Aretas IV, ruler of Nabatea, to the east, he quickly divorced her in favor of Herodias. In one dicey move, Antipas had stolen his brother's wife, compromised his eastern border, and alienated his Jewish subjects, whose law forbade wife-swapping, especially among brothers. But with Herodias beside him, Herod Antipas must have thought himself powerful enough to manage the consequences.

But neither Antipas nor Herodias had expected their transgression to become a matter of public agitation. After all, who was there to agitate, except the usual ragtag band of upstarts? A real prophet had not troubled Israel for more than four hundred years.

But trouble was edging toward them in the form of a new Elijah, whom God had been nurturing with locusts and honey in the wilderness that bordered their realm. This prophet, John the Baptist, cared nothing for diplomacy. He could not be bought or bullied, and was preaching a message of repentance to all who would listen: "A voice of one calling in the desert, 'Prepare the way for the Lord, make straight paths for him'" (Mark 1:3).

John the Baptist spared no one, not the ordinary people who flocked to him in the desert, not the self-righteous Pharisees nor the privileged Sadducees, and certainly not Herod Antipas or Herodias, whom he upbraided for their unlawful marriage. Herodias would have liked for Antipas to kill John, yet even he had to step carefully, lest he ignite an uprising among John's ever-growing number of followers. That would be all the excuse his former father-in-law, Aretas, would need in order to attack Antipas's eastern flank. So, according to Jewish historian Josephus, John was shut up in Machaerus, a fortress just east of the Dead Sea.

On Herod Antipas's birthday a feast was held in his honor and attended by a "who's who" list of dignitaries. During the evening, Herodias's young daughter, Salome, performed a dance for Herod Antipas and his guests which so pleased him that he promised his step-daughter anything she desired, up to half his kingdom.

Ever the good daughter, Salome hastened to her mother for advice. Should she request a splendid palace or a portion of the royal treasury? But Herodias had one thing only in mind. When Salome returned to the banquet hall, Salome surprised Antipas with a gruesome demand: "I want you to give me, right now, the head of John the Baptist on a platter."

Though Herod Antipas was distressed by her request, he was even more distressed at the prospect of breaking an oath he had so publicly made. Therefore, in complete disregard for Jewish law, which prohibited both execution without trial and decapitation as a form of execution, he immediately ordered John's death.

That night, Herodias must have savored her triumph over the man whom Jesus referred to as the greatest who had yet lived. John had been sent as the last of the prophets, a new Elijah, whose preaching was to prepare the way for Jesus. Had Herodias heeded John's call to repentance, her heart might have welcomed the gospel. Rather than being remembered as just one more member of a bloody dynasty, she could have become a true child of God. Instead of casting her lot with the great women of the Bible, however, she chose to model herself on one of the worst—Jezebel, her spiritual mother. By so doing, she sealed her heart against the truth and all the transforming possibilities of grace.

Her Legacy of Prayer

For John had been saying to Herod, "It is not lawful for you to have your brother's wife." So Herodias nursed a grudge against John and wanted to kill him.

—*Mark 6:18–19*

REFLECT ON: Mark 6:14–29.

PRAISE GOD: That he gives us opportunities to repent and turn back to him.

OFFER THANKS: For the men and women in your own life who have had the courage to tell you the truth.

CONFESS: Any tendency to respond defensively to constructive criticism.

ASK GOD: For the grace to respond to correction with humility.

Lift Your Heart

*M*ost of us hate criticism. Part of our defensiveness stems from our inability to see the connection between brokenness and grace. How differently we would respond if we understood that repentance is like a garden hoe breaking up the soil to make it ready for the seed. If we want to cultivate the fruit of the Spirit in our lives—love, joy, peace, patience, kindness, goodness, faithfulness, gentleness, and self-control—

we must cherish the truth, however it comes to us. Being receptive to criticism doesn't mean we become women with low self-esteem. It simply means that we will be open about our sins and faults, believing in God's desire to forgive and help us to change. This week, take some time for a little soul-searching. Is God trying to get your attention about something that is off-kilter in your own life? Is he raising up a prophet in your own family—a child or husband who is trying to tell you the truth? If so, listen, and then pray about what you hear. Resist the temptation to make the person pay for his or her words by sulking, holding a grudge, or criticizing him or her in turn. Instead, be the first to say you're sorry. A habit of repentance will make your heart fertile soil for God's grace.

Father, I know how deceitful the human heart can be. Please give me the courage to be honest and the faith to believe in your forgiveness. May my heart become a place of brokenness, where grace and truth can flourish.

— 43 —

JOANNA

Her Name Means
"The Lord Gives Graciously"

HER CHARACTER:	A woman of high rank in Herod's court, she experienced healing at Jesus' hands. She responded by giving herself totally, supporting his ministry, and following him wherever he went. The story of her healing may have been known to Herod himself.
HER JOY:	To find the tomb empty except for the angels who proclaimed Jesus alive.
KEY SCRIPTURES:	Luke 8:1–3; 24:10 (and Matthew 14:1–12 and Luke 23:7–12 for background on Herod and his court)

Joanna was a wealthy woman, accustomed to an atmosphere of worldliness. One didn't live in Herod Antipas's courts without learning to navigate the powerful currents of intrigue that swirled continuously around his throne. But nothing had so troubled and sickened her as the death of the prophet John. A holy man murdered for speaking the plain truth, his head was carried to Herodias on a platter, like a tantalizing dish to satisfy her appetite for revenge. How sad she had been as she watched Jesus grieving his cousin's murder.

Joanna's own life had been so altered by Christ that she may have hoped to influence Herod on his behalf. Married to Cuza, the manager of Herod's vast estates, she was well-positioned for the task. How intently Herod would have listened as she recounted the details of her miraculous healing. But after John's death, Joanna must have wondered what would become of Jesus should he ever have the misfortune of falling into Herod's hands. And what, for that matter, would become of his followers?

Though Joanna would have realized the escalating risks that faith required, there is not the slightest evidence she flinched from them. Unlike Nicodemus, she made no effort to hide her admiration for Jesus. Along with other women, she provided for his needs from her own purse. Perhaps her gifts made it just a little easier on this teacher who had no place to lay his head (Matthew 8:20).

All we really know of Joanna, in addition to her status as Cuza's wife, is that Jesus cured her of some spiritual or physical malady, that she was among a group of women who traveled with Jesus and his disciples, that she supported his ministry out of her own means, and that she was present at the Resurrection along with Mary Magdalene and Mary the mother of James. Whether her faith cost her dearly or little in either her marriage or at court is a matter for speculation.

But certainly Joanna would have known that Herod had mocked the Lord prior to his execution at Pilate's hands. Quite probably she was among the women present at the Crucifixion. And like the others who went to the tomb to anoint his body, she must have fallen on her face in awe of the angels who greeted her with astonishing news: "Why do you look for the living among the dead? He is not here; he has risen! Remember how he told you, while he was still with you in Galilee: The Son of Man must be delivered into the hands of sinful men, be crucified and on the third day be raised again" (Luke 24:5).

She would have run with the others to tell the disciples of the incredible discovery. Though Peter and the other disciples discounted the story as the ravings of hysterical women, Joanna would hardly have doubted herself. For she was a woman who lived in an atmosphere of power. She had just witnessed a far greater power than Herod's or even

Pilate's, and she would have recognized it as the same power that had healed her.

It didn't matter that her husband served a man who had humiliated Christ; Joanna knew where her allegiance belonged. A woman of high rank, she became part of the intimate circle of Christ's followers, casting her lot with fishermen and poor people rather than with the rich and the powerful. God honored her by making her one of the first witnesses of the Resurrection.

Her Legacy of Prayer

> *Remember how he told you, while he was still with you in Galilee:*
> *"The Son of Man must be delivered into the hands of sinful men, be*
> *crucified and on the third day be raised again."*
>
> *—Luke 24:6–7*

REFLECT ON: Luke 24:1–12.

PRAISE GOD: For the truth the psalmist proclaims: "The wicked plot against the righteous and gnash their teeth at them; but the LORD laughs at the wicked, for he knows their day is coming" (Psalm 37:12–13).

OFFER THANKS: That the ultimate victory is God's—and ours!

CONFESS: Any tendency to believe that God is well-intentioned but weak.

ASK GOD: For a greater sense of his majesty.

Lift Your Heart

*H*andel's *Messiah*, a traditional Christmas favorite, is worth listening to all year round. Handel wrote his masterpiece in just twenty-four days, while on the verge of being thrown into debtors' prison. When he finished the movement that became known as the "Hallelujah Chorus," he turned to his servant with tears streaming down his face and exclaimed, "I did think I did see all heaven before me, and the great God himself." This week, consider purchasing a recording of the *Messiah*. As you listen to the lyrics and the music, ask for the grace to "see all heaven before you, and the great God himself."

Lord, you laugh at the rulers and powers of this world who oppose you. Help me to realize that no evil, regardless of how terrible or prolonged it might be, can ever stand against you. Give me a greater sense of your resurrection power and majesty.

44

THE SYROPHOENICIAN WOMAN

HER CHARACTER:	Though a Gentile, she addressed Jesus as "Lord, Son of David." Her great faith resulted in her daughter's deliverance.
HER SORROW:	That her child was possessed by an evil spirit.
HER JOY:	That Jesus freed her daughter from spiritual bondage.
KEY SCRIPTURES:	Matthew 15:21–28; Mark 7:24–30

Her body jerked and twisted, arms thrashing the air. Wide-eyed, the little girl spoke to ghosts her mother could not see, her face changing as rapidly as clouds in a sudden storm. Fear, surprise, and then a crazy kind of laughter blew through her, as though someone had stolen her soul. Dark hair stuck in gummy strands against her cheeks.

Her mother wondered what had become of the sweet child who had followed her like a puppy wherever she went. How she missed those soft kisses and the button nose that had nuzzled her cheek. She had hardly slept these last few nights for fear of what her daughter might do to herself. Neither of them, she thought, could stand much more.

Just that morning she had caught wind of a Jewish healer who, friends said, had come to Tyre hoping for relief from the crowds that mobbed him in Galilee. It didn't matter that Jews seldom mingled with Gentiles. She would go to him, beg his help, throw a fit herself if necessary. She would do whatever it took to get him to listen. It didn't take long to find him.

She approached Jesus, pleading, "Lord, Son of David, have mercy on me! My daughter is suffering terribly from demon-possession."

But Jesus ignored the woman, making no reply.

Finally, his disciples said to Jesus, "Send her away, for she keeps crying out after us."

But Jesus knew it would not be that easy to get rid of her. The only way, in fact, would be to answer her prayer. He told them, "I was sent only to the lost sheep of Israel."

Hearing him, the woman fell at his feet again, imploring, "Lord, help me!"

Then Jesus turned and said, "It is not right to take the children's bread and toss it to their dogs."

But the woman would not give up. "Yes, Lord," she said, "but even the dogs eat the crumbs that fall from their masters' table."

"Woman, you have great faith! Your request is granted," Jesus said.

So the Syrophoenician woman returned to her daughter, who was delivered from the evil spirit the very same hour that Jesus had spoken.

Scripture doesn't describe the little girl of this story in any detail; it says only that she was possessed by a demon. But judging from similar incidents, such as that of the Gerasene demoniac, whose story is told in Luke 8, or the little boy in Matthew 17 who kept throwing himself into the fire, the signs of demonic possession were probably both obvious and frightening.

But why did Jesus seem so rude to the poor woman, ignoring her request and then referring to her and her child as dogs?

His response may sound a little less harsh when you realize that the word he used for "dogs" was not the derisive one Jews ordinarily reserved for Gentiles. Instead, it was the term used for little dogs kept as pets. Jesus was also making it clear that his primary mission was to the Israelites. Had Jesus performed healings and miracles in Tyre and Sidon, he would have risked the same kind of mob scenes he had just left behind in Galilee, thus inaugurating a ministry to the Gentiles in advance of his Father's timing.

The woman couldn't have known the reason for his silence, however, and it must have tested her faith. But rather than give up or take offense, she exercised her quick wit, revealing both a deep humility and a tenacious faith. It was a combination Jesus seemed unable to resist— fertile soil in which to grow a miracle. The Syrophoenician woman must have rejoiced that day to see the daughter she loved safe and sane, grateful for the life-giving bread that had fallen from the Master's table.

Her Legacy of Prayer

Then Jesus answered, "Woman, you have great faith! Your request is granted."

—*Matthew 15:28*

REFLECT ON: Matthew 15:21–28.

PRAISE GOD: For his power to deliver us from every form of evil.

OFFER THANKS: For the deliverance you have already experienced.

CONFESS: Any hopelessness about your children or others you love.

ASK GOD: To give you the same "terrier-like" faith that the Syrophoenician woman had, so that you will never give up praying for the salvation of your loved ones.

Lift Your Heart

$\mathcal{T}$hough most of our children will never suffer from actual demonic possession, all of them are engaged, as we are, in a spiritual battle. As a mother, your prayers and your life play a role in the spiritual protection of your children. This week, pray Psalm 46 or Psalm 91 for the spiritual protection of your family. Or take a few moments to pray these verses from Psalm 125:

> *Those who trust in the LORD are like Mount Zion,*
> *   which cannot be shaken but endures forever.*
> *As the mountains surround Jerusalem,*
> *   so the LORD surrounds his people*
> *   both now and forevermore.*

Imagine that every member of your family is surrounded by God, just as mountains surround the city of Jerusalem. Offer each one to him, placing them in his care. When you are worried about a particular family member, pray a quick prayer asking God to surround him or her with his protection.

Lord, surround my children like the mountains surrounding Jerusalem. Encircle our family with your power and peace. Deliver us from evil now and forever. Amen.

45

MARTHA

Her Name, the Feminine Form
of "Lord," Means "Lady"

HER CHARACTER:	Active and pragmatic, she seemed never at a loss for words. Though Jesus chastened her for allowing herself to become worried and upset by small things, she remained his close friend and follower.
HER SORROW:	To have waited, seemingly in vain, for Jesus to return in time to heal her brother, Lazarus.
HER JOY:	To watch as Jesus restored her brother to life.
KEY SCRIPTURES:	Luke 10:38–42; John 11:1–12:3

Martha, Mary, and their brother, Lazarus, lived together in Bethany, a village just two miles from Jerusalem, on the eastern slope of the Mount of Olives. All three were intimate friends of Jesus.

During one of his frequent stays in their home, Martha became annoyed with Mary, her indignation spilling over like water from a boiling pot. Instead of helping with the considerable chore of feeding and housing Jesus and his retinue of disciples, Mary had been spending her time sitting happily at his feet. Feeling ignored and unappreciated, Martha marched over to Jesus and demanded: "Lord, don't you care that my sister has left me to do the work by myself? Tell her to help me!"

But Jesus wouldn't oblige. Instead, he chided her, "Martha, Martha, you are worried and upset about many things, but only one thing is needed. Mary has chosen what is better, and it will not be taken away from her."

Jesus' tender rebuke must have embarrassed and startled her, calcu lated as it was to break the grip of her self-pity and reveal what was really taking place under her own roof and in her own heart. Perhaps this competent woman realized for the first time just how much she had been missing. Distracted by the need to serve Jesus, she had not taken time to enjoy him, to listen and learn from him. Her anger at Mary may have stemmed more from envy than from any concern about being overworked, for her sister had made her way into the circle of men to sit at the feet of the Teacher and learn from him.

Martha's story, of course, points to what is really important in life. She seemed confused and distracted, conned into believing her cease-less activity would produce something of lasting importance. But Martha does more than simply instruct through her mistakes. She shows what it is like to have a relationship with Jesus so solid and close that no posturing or hiding is necessary. Martha seemed free to be her-self in his presence. Where else should she have taken her frustration and anger, after all, but to Jesus?

Martha seems to have worked out her faith directly and actively, questioning, challenging, asking Jesus to rectify whatever had gone wrong. Her spirituality was like that of Jacob, who wrestled all night with an angel, or Job, who questioned God in the midst of his suf-fering, or Peter, who stumbled brashly forward into faith despite his mistakes.

In a later scene, after her brother died, we see Martha running to meet Jesus as soon as she heard he was near. Her greeting to Jesus was tinged with complaint: "Lord, if you had been here, my brother would not have died." But faith, too, was present: "I know that even now God will give you whatever you ask."

"Your brother will rise again," Jesus assured her.

"I know he will rise again in the resurrection at the last day," Martha replied.

"I am the resurrection and the life," Jesus said. "He who believes in me will live, even though he dies; and whoever lives and believes in me will never die. Do you believe this?"

"Yes, Lord," she told him. "I believe that you are the Christ, the Son of God, who was to come into the world."

But right after her tremendous expression of faith, Martha's practical side reasserted itself. When Jesus asked for the stone to be removed from Lazarus's tomb, she objected, raising the concern on everyone's mind: "But, Lord, by this time there is a bad odor, for he has been there four days!" How amazed she must have been when instead of the stench of death, Lazarus himself emerged from the tomb.

The more we delve into Martha's story, the more familiar it seems—as familiar as the face gazing at us in the bathroom mirror. A woman who placed too much importance on her own activity and not enough on sitting quietly before Jesus, she pleaded for fairness without realizing that her version of fairness was itself unfair. Her commonsensical approach to life made faith difficult. But she also loved Jesus and was confident of his love for her. How else could she have found the courage to keep pressing him for answers to her many questions? Martha offers a warmly human portrait of what it meant to have Jesus as a friend, allowing him to stretch her faith, rebuke her small vision of the world, and show her what the power of God could do.

Her Legacy of Prayer .

> *"Lord, don't you care that my sister has left me to do the work by myself? Tell her to help me!"*
> —*Luke 10:40*

REFLECT ON: Luke 10:38–41.

PRAISE GOD: For his patience.

OFFER THANKS: That God meets us where we are rather than where we "should be."

CONFESS: Any tendency to resent other women in your life.

ASK GOD: For the grace to be completely honest with him.

Lift Your Heart

*M*artha took her complaint about her sister directly to Jesus. Is someone in your life causing you trouble—your daughter, mother, coworker, sister in faith, even a rival? Rather than expressing your grievance to anyone who will listen, take your complaint directly to God. Tell him everything that's bothering you. Ask him to give you understanding about how to respond to this person, even if it means that you, not she, are the one who needs to change.

———————————

Father, you know how difficult it is for me to relate to _____. Please help me to know what you think of our difficulties. I ask you for the grace to let go of my own sense of hurt and grievance. If you want me to do anything at all to try to improve the situation, make me sensitive and obedient to your guidance.

46

MARY
OF BETHANY

Her Name May Mean "Bitterness"

HER CHARACTER:	Mary appears to have been a single woman, totally devoted to Jesus. The gospel portrays her, by way of contrast with her sister, Martha, as a woman of few words. As Jesus neared the time of his triumphal entry into Jerusalem prior to Passover, she performed a gesture of great prophetic significance, one that offended Judas Iscariot, the disciple who betrayed Jesus.
HER SORROW:	She wept at the tomb of her brother, Lazarus, and must have experienced great sorrow at the death of Jesus.
HER JOY:	To have done something beautiful for Jesus.
KEY SCRIPTURES:	Matthew 26:6–13; Mark 14:3–9; Luke 10:38–42; John 11:1–12:11

erusalem was swollen with a hundred thousand worshipers, pilgrims who had come to celebrate the annual Passover feast. Every one of them, it seemed, had heard tales of the rabbi Jesus.

"I wouldn't have believed it myself if I hadn't been there," one man exclaimed. "I assure you, Lazarus drew his last breath a full four days before the Nazarene ever arrived."

"My cousin saw the whole thing," said another. "According to her, Jesus simply shouted his name and Lazarus came out of the tomb, still bound in his grave clothes."

"I hear the rabbi is coming to Jerusalem to be crowned king during Passover," said the first man.

"Better if he stayed home," said another. "The chief priests say the whole story is nonsense, that Jesus is a rabble-rouser who'll soon have the Romans up in arms against us all."

The rumors spread quickly as people speculated about whether Jesus would return for the Passover celebration. And all the while they kept chasing after Mary, inquiring about her brother. Had he really been dead four days? Didn't he smell when he came stumbling out of the tomb? What was it like to live in the same house with a ghost? Did he eat and sleep? Could you see straight through him? Did he simply float through the air wherever he went? Was it a sham, a show, a miracle?

She could hardly blame them for their crazy questions. Why shouldn't they be curious about the amazing event that had taken place in Bethany several weeks earlier? How could they know that Lazarus was as normal as any other living man? After all, raising people from the dead wasn't your everyday kind of miracle. These days she felt a rush of joy run through her, like wine overflowing a cup, whenever she looked at Lazarus. Her own flesh and blood had been called out of darkness by a man who was filled with light. How she longed to see Jesus again.

But shadows framed the edges of her happiness. No amount of celebrating could erase the memory of Jesus as he wept that day outside her brother's tomb. Even as others were celebrating the most spectacular miracle imaginable, he seemed strangely quiet. What was he thinking as he gazed at them? she wondered. She wished he would tell her, that she could plumb the secrets of his heart.

When Jesus finally returned to Bethany before the Passover, Martha served a feast in his honor. As Jesus was reclining at the table with the other guests, Mary entered the room and anointed his head with a pint of expensive perfume. Its fragrance filled the whole house.

The disciple Judas Iscariot, failing to appreciate her gesture, objected strenuously. "Why wasn't this perfume sold and the money given to the poor? It was worth a year's wages." Though he actually cared nothing for the destitute, Judas was the keeper of the common purse, a man always looking for a chance to fatten his own pockets.

But rather than scolding Mary for her extravagance, Jesus praised her, saying, "Why are you bothering this woman? She has done a beautiful thing to me. The poor you will always have with you, but you will not always have me. When she poured this perfume on my body, she did it to prepare me for burial. I tell you the truth, whenever this gospel is preached throughout the world, what she has done will also be told, in memory of her."

From her first encounter with Jesus, Mary seems to have pursued one thing above all—the deepest possible relationship with him. She soaked up his teaching, took his promises to heart, listened for every change of inflection that would yield more clues about him. Love gave her insights that others missed. Somehow, she must have understood that Jesus would not enter Jerusalem to lasting acclaim but to death and dishonor. For a time, the light itself would appear to be smothered by the darkness. While everyone else was busy celebrating Jesus' triumph in raising Lazarus, Mary stood quietly beside him, sharing his grief.

Jesus found Mary's extravagant act of adoration a beautiful thing, assuring everyone that she would be remembered forever for the way she lavished herself upon him. Mary of Bethany was a woman unafraid of expressing her love, determined to seek the heart of God, a prophet whose gesture speaks eloquently even from a distance of two thousand years.

Her Legacy of Prayer

"Why are you bothering this woman? She has done a beautiful thing to me."

—*Matthew 26:10*

REFLECT ON:	Matthew 26:6–13.
PRAISE GOD:	For giving us the ability to please him.
OFFER THANKS.	For all the beautiful things God has done for you.
CONFESS:	Any unwillingness to embrace the difficult parts of the gospel as well as the joyful parts.
ASK GOD:	To give you a greater hunger to live in his presence and to seek his face.

Lift Your Heart

Lovers like nothing better than to please their beloved. Mother Teresa of Calcutta was a woman who loved God extravagantly. Famous for her work with the poorest of the poor in India and throughout the world, she was always looking for a chance to do "something beautiful for God." How easy it is for us to neglect our Divine Lover by always asking him to do beautiful things for us rather than by developing our own capacity to please and delight him. You don't have to travel to the other side of the world to find opportunities to do something beautiful for God. Look for him in the poorest of the poor in your own community— those who are emotionally impoverished, isolated, ill. Find a way to bring the light of God's love into their darkness. Spend time simply praising God for who he is and how he has revealed himself to you. Honor him by giving him something precious in your own life. Even the smallest gesture can become a beautiful gift for God.

Lord, you have done so many beautiful things for me, pursuing me when I cared nothing for you, restoring my hope, giving me a future worth living for. I want to offer myself generously—not as a miser doling out her favors in hope of a return, but as a woman completely in love with her Maker. Make my life a sweet-smelling fragrance to please you.

47

SALOME, MOTHER OF THE ZEBEDEES

Her Name, the Feminine Form
of Solomon, Means "Peace"

HER CHARACTER:	A devoted follower of Jesus, whose husband ran a fishing business, she shared the common misconception that the Messiah would drive out the Romans and establish a literal kingdom in Palestine. Her name was probably Salome.
HER SORROW:	To have stood with other women at the cross, witnessing the death of Jesus of Nazareth.
HER JOY:	To have seen an angel at Christ's tomb, who proclaimed the Resurrection.
KEY SCRIPTURES:	Matthew 20:20–24; 27:56; Mark 15:40–41; 16:1–2

Salome loved Jesus nearly as much as her own two sons, James and John. She would never forget the day they left their father and their fishing nets to follow him. Lately, she, too, had come to believe that Jesus was the Messiah of God.

She had smiled when she heard Jesus had nicknamed them "the Sons of Thunder." Surely he had recognized the seeds of greatness in the two feisty brothers from Capernaum. Why else would he have invited them into his inner circle, along with Simon Peter? She had heard how Jesus had led the three up a high mountain. When they came down, her garrulous sons could hardly speak. But then the story came out.

"Jesus' face was blindingly bright like the sun. . . .

"Moses and Elijah appeared and spoke with him. . . .

"Suddenly a cloud surrounded us and a voice from heaven said, 'This is my Son, whom I love; with him I am well pleased. Listen to him!'" (Mark 9:3–7).

Salome had listened. She had seen the glory and the power that radiated from the man. Though she had heard ominous rumors that Jerusalem's men of power hated Jesus, she also knew that the great King David had faced his own share of enemies before establishing his kingdom. And hadn't Jesus promised his disciples that they would sit on twelve thrones in his kingdom? "Everyone who has left houses or brothers or sisters or father or mother or children or fields for my sake," he had said, "will receive a hundred times as much and will inherit eternal life" (Mark 10:30). How could she doubt him? Even with faith small as a mustard seed, mountains could be moved.

Salome had left behind her comfortable home on the northwest shore of Galilee to join her sons. Now, as they journeyed up to Jerusalem, she remembered other words Jesus had spoken: "Ask and it will be given to you; seek and you will find; knock and the door will be opened to you" (Matthew 7:7). She would no longer deny herself the one favor her heart desired. Prostrating herself before him, she begged, "Grant that one of these two sons of mine may sit at your right and the other at your left in your kingdom."

But instead of replying to her, Jesus turned to James and John and said, "You don't know what you are asking. Can you drink the cup I am going to drink?"

"We can," they answered.

Jesus said to them, "You will indeed drink from my cup, but to sit at my right or left is not for me to grant. These places belong to those for whom they have been prepared by my Father."

Jesus, who knew Zebedee's sons better than anyone, realized that Salome was only voicing their rising ambitions. Like any loving mother, she had simply asked for what she thought would make her children happy. But as Jesus' reply and subsequent events proved, this mother didn't begin to comprehend what she was asking. Soon, the man she had approached as a king would himself die on a cross. And she would be one of the women who witnessed his death.

After it was over, Salome may have remembered the anguished faces of the men who had been crucified with Jesus, one on his right hand and the other on his left—an ironic reminder of her request on the way up to Jerusalem. Such a memory would only have increased her terror for what might now happen to her sons.

Along with other faithful women at the cross, Salome was present on the morning of the Resurrection. Surely the angel's words—"He has risen! He is not here!"—would have comforted her later in life (assuming she was still alive) when her son James became the first martyred apostle, dying at the hands of Herod Agrippa.

Instead of asking Jesus what he wanted for her sons, Salome acted as though she knew exactly what he needed to do on their behalf. She must have forgotten that Jesus had exhorted his followers to leave behind not only houses, brothers and sisters, fathers and mothers for his sake, but also children. In Salome's case, it didn't mean turning her back on her children but surrendering them to God. It meant putting Jesus above everything and everyone, loving him better than her own sons. Only then would she understand the meaning of what they would suffer as followers of Christ. Only then would she really know how to pray.

Her Legacy of Prayer

> *"Grant that one of these two sons of mine may sit at your right and the other at your left in your kingdom."*
>
> —*Matthew 20:21*

REFLECT ON:	Matthew 20:20–28.
PRAISE GOD:	That his Son has shown us the true meaning of greatness.
OFFER THANKS:	For all the ways, large and small, that God has served you.
CONFESS:	Pride and misguided ambition.
ASK GOD:	For the grace to make the connection that the way down leads to the way up, that it is the humble woman who will be considered great in the kingdom.

Lift Your Heart

*M*any women have heard the message of servanthood and internalized it in unhealthy ways. Instead of realizing their inherent dignity as women, they have defined their worth primarily in terms of others. But both men and women are called to model themselves on Christ, who was not a person who suffered from low self-esteem. His humility wasn't a cover for a sense of unworthiness. If you have made the mistake of living your life through your husband or your children, ask God for the grace to change. Admit you are a human being who needs care, consideration, and replenishment. Ask God to restore balance in your life. But as you go through the process of finding balance, don't eliminate the word *humility* from your vocabulary by embracing a life of selfishness. This week, ask each day for eyes to see another's need. Then ask for grace to serve in a way that truly models the humility of Jesus.

Lord, forgive me for any pride that has crowded you out of my heart. Whenever I am tempted to think or act with selfish ambition, place a check in my spirit. Give me, instead, the courage to be a servant. Make more room in my heart for your love.

48

THE WIDOW WITH
THE TWO COINS

HER CHARACTER:	Though extremely poor, she is one of the most greathearted people in the Bible. Just after warning his disciples to watch out for the teachers of the law, who devour widows' houses, Jesus caught sight of her in the temple. He may have called attention to her as a case in point.
HER SORROW:	To be alone, without a husband to provide for her.
HER JOY:	To surrender herself to God completely, trusting him to act on her behalf.
KEY SCRIPTURES:	Mark 12:41–44; Luke 21:1–4

With Passover approaching, the temple was packed with worshipers from all over Israel. The previous Sunday, Jesus had created a sensation as he rode down the Mount of Olives and into Jerusalem, mounted on a donkey. A large crowd had gathered, carpeting the road with palm branches and shouting: "Hosanna to the Son of David! Blessed is he who comes in the name of the Lord! Hosanna in the highest."

Some of the Pharisees, scandalized that Jesus was being hailed as Messiah, demanded, "Teacher, rebuke your disciples!"

"I tell you," he replied, "if they keep quiet, the stones will cry out."

Stung by his words, the teachers of the law began to plot how they could break the law by murdering him at their first opportunity.

Days later, Jesus sat opposite the temple treasury, in the Court of the Women. The place was crowded with people dropping their offerings into one of the thirteen trumpet-shaped receptacles that hung on the walls. But Jesus had eyes for only one of them. He watched as a widow deposited two small copper coins, less than a day's wages.

Quickly, he called to his disciples, "I tell you the truth, this poor widow has put more into the treasury than all the others. They all gave out of their wealth; but she, out of her poverty, put in everything—all she had to live on."

No one else would have noticed the woman. But Jesus, with eyes that penetrated both her circumstances and her heart, recognized the astonishing nature of her gift. Her gesture was a sign of complete abandonment to God.

We know nothing of the widow except her poverty and faith. Without faith, she wouldn't have offered her last penny, believing God would care for her better than she could care for herself. But there is yet another, more subtle aspect to her story. How easy it would have been for her to conclude that her gift was simply too meager to offer. What need had God for two copper coins anyway? Surely they meant more to her than they would to him. Somehow she must have had the grace to believe in the value of her small offering.

Maybe God, in a manner of speaking, *did* need what she had to offer. Perhaps her gesture consoled Jesus a short time before his passion and death. She had given everything she had to live on; soon, he would give his very life.

The story of the widow and her two copper coins reminds us that God's kingdom works on entirely different principles than the kingdom of this world. In the divine economy, the size of the gift is of no consequence; what matters is the size of the giver's heart.

Her Legacy of Prayer

Jesus said, "I tell you the truth, this poor widow has put more into the treasury than all the others. They all gave out of their wealth; but she, out of her poverty, put in everything—all she had to live on."

—Mark 21:43

REFLECT ON: Mark 12:41–44.

PRAISE GOD: For judging not by outward appearances but as one who sees the heart.

OFFER THANKS: For blessings of money, time, energy, and emotional resources.

CONFESS: Any tendency to act as though your security depends more on you than it does on God.

ASK GOD: To make you a generous woman with the faith to believe that even small gifts are worth giving.

Lift Your Heart

This week, think of an area of your life that feels particularly empty or impoverished. You may be lonely, financially stretched, or worried about the future. Whatever it is, pray about it. Listen for the voice of the Holy Spirit. Is God inviting you to do something to express your trust? What kind of offering would be the most pleasing to him? Once you hear his voice, go ahead and give him what his heart desires.

Father, you are the source of every blessing. This week, help me to give, not only out of my wealth, but out of my poverty. Remind me that I belong to you, body and soul, heart and mind, past, present, and future.

49

MARY MAGDALENE

Her Name May Mean
"Bitterness"

HER CHARACTER:	Though mistakenly characterized as a prostitute in many popular writings, the Bible says only that Mary was possessed by seven demons. She probably suffered a serious mental or physical illness from which Jesus delivered her. She is a beautiful example of a woman whose life was poured out in response to God's extravagant grace.
HER SORROW:	To watch Jesus' agony at Calvary.
HER JOY:	To have been the first witness to the Resurrection.
KEY SCRIPTURES:	Matthew 27:56, 61; 28:1; Mark 15:40, 47; 16:1–19; Luke 8:2; 24:10; John 19:25; 20:1–18

She made her way through the shadows to the garden tomb, grateful for the darkness that shrouded her tears. How, she wondered, could the world go on as though nothing at all had happened? How could the mountains keep from crashing down, the sky resist falling? Had everyone but her lost their minds? Had no one noticed that the world had collapsed two days ago?

For the past three years she had followed the rabbi across Galilee and Judea, providing for him out of her own small purse. She had loved his hearty laughter and the smile that flashed across his face whenever he saw her. Wherever they went, she felt privileged to tell her story, grateful to be among his growing band of followers.

She had grown up in Magdala, a prosperous town on the west bank of Galilee. But she had not prospered. How could a woman thrive when she was filled with demons who controlled her mind? Though she had begged for mercy, no mercy had been given. Instead, her delusions locked her into a nightmare world, isolating her even from small pleasures and simple kindnesses.

But then Jesus had come. Like no rabbi she had ever encountered, he seemed neither afraid nor repulsed by her illness. "Mary," he had called to her, as though he had known her all her life. Despite the heat of the day, she shivered as he drew near, her stomach suddenly queasy. Though she backed away, she could feel a great light advancing toward her, forcing the darkness away. Suddenly her familiar companions were themselves begging for mercy, but no mercy was given.

Mary Magdalene, a woman possessed by seven demons, was restored to her right mind, her bondage a thing of the past. Eyes that had once been holes swallowing the light now shone like pools reflecting the sun.

Since then, everyone in Magdala had marveled at the change in her. How could Mary not love such a man? How could she not want to do everything for him? She thought she was living in heaven—to be close to Jesus; to witness healing after healing; to be stirred, surprised, and refreshed by his teaching. This, indeed, was joy to a woman unaccustomed to joy.

But Jesus had his share of enemies, she knew. Religious leaders in Jerusalem had been stung by his truth-telling, offended by his galling lack of diplomacy. Still, every trap they laid for him had failed ... until now.

They had struck suddenly, even though Jerusalem was crowded with pilgrims for Passover. The temple guard had arrested him at night and then turned him over to Roman authorities, who mocked and whipped him nearly to death. The rabbi from Galilee, who had promised the poor in spirit they would surely inherit the kingdom of heaven, was now in chains. His hunger and thirst for righteousness had left him not full, but empty and broken. Unblessed, he had become a curse, his body hanging naked on a Roman cross.

Mary had done her best to fight off the shadows that crowded near again as she waited through the awful hours of his agony, unable to look at the spectacle before her, yet unable to turn away. However hideous his suffering, she needed to be near him.

When it was over, she had watched Nicodemus and Joseph of Arimathea unfasten his body from the cross. Gently they had wrapped him in myrrh and aloes, enough for a king's burial. Finally, as the stone rolled across the tomb, sealing it shut, she had turned away.

After the Sabbath was over on the next day, Mary purchased yet more spices. Before the sun came up on Sunday, she approached the tomb. How on earth, she wondered, could she roll away the massive stone? But, to her surprise, the mouth of the tomb was already open. Strips of linen were lying on the floor and the burial cloth that had been wrapped around Jesus' head was folded up by itself. What had they done with his body? she wondered. To be cheated of this last chance of touching and caring for him was more than she could bear.

She stood outside the tomb weeping. Then, bending over, she looked inside. Two creatures in white sat on the stony shelf where the body had been laid. "Woman, why are you crying?" they asked.

"They have taken my Lord away," she said, "and I don't know where they have put him." Then she turned and saw a man studying her.

"Woman," he said, "why are you crying? Who is it you are looking for?"

Mistaking him for the gardener, she pleaded, "Sir, if you have carried him away, tell me where you have put him, and I will get him."

"Mary," he said.

Startled, she cried out, "Rabboni" (meaning Teacher).

By now the sun had risen. With it fled the darkness that had pursued her ever since she had heard the news of his arrest. Jesus, the one who had raised her from a living death, had himself risen from the dead.

Mary fell to the ground in awe, remembering the words of the prophet Isaiah: "The people walking in darkness have seen a great light; on those living in the land of the shadow of death a light has dawned." The garden that had so recently been a place of shadows and gloom now seemed green and bright, as though paradise itself had broken through.

The risen Jesus had appeared, not to rulers and kings, nor even first of all to his male disciples, but to a woman whose love had held her at the cross and led her to the grave. Mary Magdalene, a person who had been afflicted by demons, whose testimony would not have held up in court because she was a woman, was the first witness of the Resurrection. Once again, God had revealed himself to the lowly, and it would only be the humble whose hearing was sharp enough to perceive the message of his love.

Her Legacy of Prayer

Jesus said to her, "Mary." She turned toward him and cried out in Aramaic, "Rabboni!" (which means Teacher).

—*John 20:16*

REFLECT ON: John 20:1–18.

PRAISE GOD: That the Father has revealed his love so powerfully in Jesus.

OFFER THANKS: For the death and resurrection of Jesus, his Son and our Savior.

CONFESS: Your doubts about God's power or willingness to deliver you from some evil in your life.

ASK GOD: For the grace of deliverance.

Lift Your Heart

*O*ne day this week set your alarm clock so that you wake up a half hour before dawn. Find a spot where you can watch the sunrise. In the early morning shadows, tell God about some area of darkness in your own life or in the life of someone you love. Perhaps it's an illness, a persistent sin, loneliness, a troubled marriage, an addiction, or a wayward child. Whatever it is, surrender it by imagining yourself placing it in the garden tomb next to the body of Jesus. As the sun rises, meditate on that first Easter morning and remember that when Jesus walked out of the tomb you walked out with him. Ask God for the faith to wait and watch for his delivering power.

Lord, make me a woman like Mary Magdalene, who follows you not because of a legalistic understanding of her faith, but because of an overwhelming sense of gratitude and love for your own extravagant grace. Help me surrender my darkness to you and flood me with the light of your presence.

50

DORCAS

Her Name Means "Gazelle."
"Tabitha" Is Its Hebrew Equivalent

HER CHARACTER:	An inhabitant of Joppa, a town on the Mediterranean coast thirty-five miles north-west of Jerusalem, she belonged to one of the earliest Christian congregations. She was a disciple known for her practical works of mercy.
HER SORROW:	To have suffered a grave illness.
HER JOY:	To serve Jesus by serving the poor.
KEY SCRIPTURE:	Acts 9:36–43

The winds roared over the coast, piling water in noisy heaps along the rocky shoreline. But though she lay quietly in the upper room of her house near the sea, Dorcas did not hear them. Nor did she notice the waves of grief that spilled into the room from the heart of every woman present. For once she had nothing to offer, no word of comfort, no act of kindness to soften their suffering. Instead, she lay still as other women ministered to her, tenderly sponging her body clean to prepare it for burial.

As Peter approached the house, he could hear the noise of mourning, a sound more desolate than the tearing wind. Two men had summoned him from Lydda, where he had just healed a paralytic. They urged him to come quickly because one of the Lord's disciples in Joppa had died. He had come in haste, hoping to reach Dorcas before she had to be buried.

As soon as he entered the room where her body lay, the widows surrounded him with tangible evidence of the woman they had loved, weeping as they held up robes and other items Dorcas had sewn to clothe the poor. Quickly, Peter shooed them from the room, as though to clear the atmosphere of despair. Then he knelt beside her body.

As Peter prayed, he remembered an incident that had occurred in Galilee while Jesus was still alive. A synagogue ruler by the name of Jairus had fallen at the Lord's feet, begging him to come to his house, where his twelve-year-old daughter lay dying. But on the way, word came that the girl had already expired. Rather than turning back, Jesus had simply encouraged Jairus not to give in to fear but to keep believing. When they arrived, Jesus greeted the crowd of mourners, saying, "Why all this commotion and wailing? The child is not dead but asleep." The people began to ridicule him. Ignoring them, he cleared the house of everyone but his disciples and the girl's parents, took the child by the hand, and commanded, "Talitha koum!" ("Little girl, I say to you, get up!") The girl stood up immediately, and many people believed as a result.

The words Jesus had spoken on another occasion flooded Peter's mind: "I tell you the truth, anyone who has faith in me will do what I have been doing. He will do even greater things than these, because I am going to the Father." His faith rising like the wind outside, Peter addressed the dead woman, saying, "Tabitha, get up." Taking her by the hand, he actually helped her to her feet.

The next day, Dorcas stood alone on the roof of her house. The shore was littered with driftwood, trinkets from yesterday's storm. She breathed deeply, inhaling the sea's salty tang, soothed by the sound of waves lapping the rocks below. Strangely, the view looked somehow transparent, as though another world waited just behind the curtain of this one. Dorcas shaded her eyes with her hand, peering out at the sea. But she saw nothing other than the usual collection of fishing boats bobbing in the waves.

Sighing, she turned and went inside. She had things to do. Clothes to sew, bread to bake, the poor to feed and clothe. But even in the midst of her busy preparations, her longing for that other world increased, like hunger pains before a banquet. She fed that longing with her many practical acts of love.

Though we don't know what went through Peter's mind as he knelt and prayed at Dorcas's bedside, the parallels between the miracle at Joppa and the miracle at Jairus's house are striking. And though Scripture doesn't tell us how Dorcas responded to her incredible experience, it doesn't take much to imagine her joy. The story of her miracle spread throughout Joppa, leading many to believe.

Her Legacy of Prayer

Peter went with them, and when he arrived he was taken upstairs to the room. All the widows stood around him, crying and showing him the robes and other clothing that Dorcas had made while she was still with them.

—Acts 9:39

REFLECT ON: Acts 9:36–43.

PRAISE GOD: For his power over death.

OFFER THANKS: For answered prayers.

CONFESS: Any habit of limiting God's power to answer your prayer.

ASK GOD: To make you a woman whose love for God has practical ramifications for those around her.

Lift Your Heart

*I*s there a Dorcas in your life, a good man or woman who is suffering in some way? Someone, perhaps, who has been a great support in your own life? Resist the temptation to become depressed about what is happening to them and, instead, spend time this week praying in light of Dorcas's story. Let her miracle increase your faith and shape your prayers. If you have a photograph of the person, paste it to the dashboard of your car, your refrigerator, or your computer to remind you to pray. Ask God to bring light out of the darkness of their present circumstances.

Lord, show me how to pray with increasing faith, aware that your Spirit is no less powerful today than two thousand years ago. Act on behalf of your servant, and glorify your name by what you do.

51

LYDIA

*Her Name Signifies That She Was a Woman
of Lydia, a Region in Asia Minor*

HER CHARACTER:	A Gentile adherent of Judaism, she was a successful businesswoman who sold a type of cloth prized for its purple color. As head of her household, she may have been either widowed or single. So strong was her faith that her entire household followed her example and was baptized. She extended hospitality to Paul and his companions, even after their imprisonment.
HER SORROW:	To see Paul and Silas beaten and thrown into prison for the sake of the gospel she had embraced.
HER JOY:	That God's Spirit directed Paul and his companions to Macedonia, enabling her and others at Philippi to hear the gospel for the first time.
KEY SCRIPTURE:	Acts 16:6–40

The wind rustled the branches overhead until they became a swaying canopy whose shadow danced across the circle of women bowed in prayer. It didn't matter that Philippi had too few Jews to support a synagogue; the river's edge had become their place of worship, a green sanctuary where they gathered each Sabbath to pray.

Lydia listened as a stranger from Tarsus invoked the familiar words of the shema: "Hear, O Israel: The Lord our God, the Lord is one. Love the Lord your God with all your heart and with all your soul and with all your strength." Such prayers were like a gust of wind, fanning her longing. A Gentile who had come to Philippi from Asia Minor, Lydia was a prominent businesswoman who sold fine cloth to those who could afford it. Though not a Jew, she wanted to know this God powerful enough to part the sea yet tender enough to yearn for the love of his people.

Paul did not stop with the traditional shema; instead, he spoke of a God whose Son, Jesus, had been murdered for love. This Jesus had risen from his grave after suffering the most agonizing death imaginable. He was Messiah, the merciful and holy one who had come to save God's people.

The women sat quietly as Paul told the story. Even the branches overhead had stopped their noisy rustling. How then, Lydia wondered, was it that she felt a strong wind rushing through her? Tears rolled down her cheeks even though she felt like singing. Afterward, she and her household were baptized in the Gangites River, near Philippi. Lydia insisted that Paul and Silas (and probably Timothy and Luke) accept her hospitality. Her home may have become the very center of the church in Philippi.

Philippi seemed an unlikely place to plant the gospel. It had been named for Philip II, father of Alexander the Great, who had been attracted by gold-bearing mountains to the north of the city. Now a prosperous Roman colony located on the main highway linking the eastern provinces to Rome, its citizens included large numbers of retired Roman soldiers. Despite its size, however, Philippi hadn't even enough Jews to provide the requisite quorum of ten reliable males to form a synagogue—and it had always been Paul's habit to preach first in the synagogue. Even so, Philippi did have its group of praying women.

Interestingly, Paul had not planned to visit Philippi but had been on his way to Asia when he felt constrained by the Holy Spirit to turn aside. Soon afterward, he had a vision in which a man of Macedonia begged him, "Come over to Macedonia and help us." Days later, he found himself on the riverbank preaching to the women who had gathered there for prayer.

Shortly after Lydia's conversion, she heard news that her house-guests, Paul and Silas, had been whipped and thrust into prison. Paul's crime had been to drive an evil spirit from a slave girl who had been harassing them. Upset at the loss of profits from her fortune-telling, the girl's owners dragged Paul and Silas before the city magistrates, claiming, "These men are Jews and are throwing our city into an uproar by advocating customs unlawful for us Romans to accept or practice."

That night, with their feet in stocks, Paul and Silas prayed and sang hymns to God while the other prisoners listened. About midnight an earthquake shook the foundations of the prison so violently that the doors flew open and the chains of all the prisoners fell off. As a result, the jailer and his whole household were converted. After he was released, Paul returned to Lydia's home for a short while.

When Lydia said good-bye to the apostle and his companions as they continued on their missionary journey, she may have remembered the words of his accusers: "These men are throwing our city into an uproar." Indeed, God had thrown the entire region into an uproar from which it would never recover.

Lydia has the distinction of being Paul's first convert in Europe and the first member of the church at Philippi, a community which later became a source of great consolation to the apostle when he was imprisoned. Perhaps her prayers, joined with those of the other women gathered at the riverbank, helped prepare the way for the gospel to be planted in Europe.

Her Legacy of Prayer

On the Sabbath we went outside the city gate to the river, where we expected to find a place of prayer. We sat down and began to speak to the women who had gathered there.

—Acts 16:13

REFLECT ON:	Acts 16:6–14.
PRAISE GOD:	For sending messengers of the gospel.
OFFER THANKS:	That God enables us to believe by first opening our hearts to faith.
CONFESS:	Any way you may have neglected prayer, especially in community with other believers.
ASK GOD:	To help you make prayer a greater priority in your life.

Lift Your Heart

$\mathcal{I}$t's interesting to note that the Holy Spirit directed Paul to Macedonia and, ultimately, to a group of women who had already gathered for prayer. It almost seems as though the women's faithfulness in prayer was a magnet that attracted God's Spirit. This week, invite a few friends to pray with you. Gather in your home or find your own "green sanctuary" outdoors. Sing hymns and ask God for a fresh outpouring of his Spirit in your churches, homes, neighborhoods, and nation. Pray for a greater opening for the gospel. Perhaps God will create an "uproar" in your city as a result of your prayers.

———————————

Lord, Scripture says that you inhabit the praises of your people. Come now and dwell with us as we seek your face. Let the fresh wind of your Holy Spirit fall on us. May our churches, homes, and neighborhoods become places of prayer, shaking the world around us in a way that brings you glory.

52

PRISCILLA

Her Name, the Diminutive of "Prisca,"
Means "Worthy" or "Venerable"

HER CHARACTER:	One of the first missionaries and a leader of the early church, along with her husband, Aquila, she risked her life for the apostle Paul. Priscilla was a woman whose spiritual maturity and understanding of the faith helped build up the early church.
HER SORROW:	To experience opposition to the gospel from both Jews and Gentiles.
HER JOY:	To spread the gospel and nurture the church.
KEY SCRIPTURES:	Acts 18–19; Romans 16:3–4; 1 Corinthians 16:19; 2 Timothy 4:19

ow good it was to have Paul back again, she thought. Ephesus was on fire with the gospel, their young church growing stronger each day. Paul's preaching and miracles had brought many to faith. Even the touch of his handkerchief had healed illnesses and delivered people from evil spirits.

Priscilla couldn't help laughing when she heard the story of Sceva's seven sons, Jewish exorcists who had tried to duplicate such wonders by driving out an evil spirit with a magic invocation: "In the name of Jesus, whom Paul preaches, I command you to come out."

234

But the spirit had merely mocked them: "Jesus I know and I know about Paul, but who are you?" Then the man they were trying to deliver beat them so soundly they ran bleeding and naked from the house.

The Ephesians were so impressed by what had happened that a number of sorcerers held a public bonfire to destroy their scrolls. Their magical formulations and incantations seemed like useless trinkets in light of the greater power of Jesus.

But despite the progress of the gospel, Priscilla was aware of growing opposition. One day, she heard the sounds of a crowd forming in the streets. A silversmith was shouting to other craftsmen, who made their living selling miniature images of the many-breasted goddess Artemis: "Men, you know we receive a good income from this business. And you see and hear how this fellow Paul has convinced and led astray large numbers of people here in Ephesus and in practically the whole province of Asia. He says that man-made gods are no gods at all. There is danger not only that our trade will lose its good name, but also that the temple of the great goddess Artemis will be discredited, and the goddess herself, who is worshiped throughout the province of Asia and the world, will be robbed of her divine majesty."

The crowd erupted into a riot, seizing two of Paul's companions. Priscilla was distressed when Paul insisted on addressing the mob. She was certain such boldness could only end in further violence. With her husband's help, she was able to restrain him until a city official calmed the crowd and it dispersed. Soon after, Paul set out to spread the gospel in Macedonia.

Though the book of Acts describes the riot in Ephesus, it does not tell us that either Priscilla or Aquila were actually present, only that some disciples prevented Paul from entering the fray, possibly saving his life in the process. Since Priscilla and her husband were leaders of the church in Ephesus, it is quite possible they were among those who intervened on Paul's behalf.

Priscilla's faith had been planted years earlier in an atmosphere of strife and controversy, first in Rome and later in Corinth. The latter was a commercial center famous for its appetite for vice, hardly a place to nurture the faith of a new believer. Yet that was where God transplanted her, along with her husband, Aquila, after Claudius expelled Jews from Rome in A.D. 49, tired of their constant fighting about Chrestus (a probable reference to Christ).

Though various gods were worshiped in Corinth, none was more popular than Aphrodite, the Greek goddess of love, whose temple at one time boasted more than a thousand sacred prostitutes. Throughout the empire, the phrase "Corinthian girl" was just another name for "prostitute."

After the couple had been in Corinth for about a year, they met up with a man who would involve them in yet more controversy. Paul of Tarsus was a Jew who had ruthlessly persecuted Jesus' followers until his own dramatic conversion. Lately, he had been traveling in Asia Minor and Macedonia, preaching the gospel wherever he went. When he arrived in Corinth, he probably met the couple through their common trade as tentmakers. Priscilla and Aquila invited Paul to stay in their home and work with them. As always, Paul preached the gospel first in the local synagogue and then to the Gentiles. And, as always, his preaching generated both faith and opposition. After eighteen months, leading Jews of Corinth hauled him before the proconsul to accuse him of spreading an illicit religion. After the charge was dismissed, Paul set sail for Ephesus, taking Priscilla and Aquila with him.

The three missionaries must have been eager to see a city that ranked in importance with Rome, Corinth, Antioch, and Alexandria. The capital of provincial Asia, Ephesus boasted a temple to Artemis (also known as Diana) so enormous that it was considered one of the seven wonders of the ancient world. After only a short while, Paul left for other ports, leaving the couple behind to lead the church that met in their home.

Before long another Jew arrived, preaching eloquently about Jesus to the Jews at Ephesus. But Apollos, a native of Alexandria, had grasped only a shadow of the gospel, one more in keeping with the message of John the Baptist than of Jesus. Rather than denouncing him for his inadequate presentation, Priscilla and Aquila merely took him aside and instructed him in the faith. They did their job so well, in fact, that believers in Ephesus eventually sent the gifted preacher to Corinth, where he advanced the work Paul had begun.

Priscilla must have been a spiritually mature woman whose gifts equipped her for leadership. Her name actually precedes Aquila's four out of the six times they are mentioned in the New Testament, probably signifying her greater abilities as a leader or the fact that her family may have hailed from a higher social strata than his. Whatever the case, Priscilla's role in instructing Apollos and leading the early church is remarkable.

Along with Aquila, she was the best friend Paul could have had, helping him establish the church and risking her life for his sake. Paul mentions the couple's courage in one of his letters but doesn't elaborate on the circumstances.

Rather than withering in the soil of controversy, Priscilla's faith seemed to flourish. She helped establish the early church in an atmosphere of great hostility, risking her own life for the sake of the gospel she loved.

Her Legacy of Prayer

> *Greet Priscilla and Aquila, my fellow workers in Christ Jesus. They risked their lives for me. Not only I but all the churches of the Gentiles are grateful to them.*
>
> —*Romans 16:3–4*

REFLECT ON:	Acts 18:18–28.
PRAISE GOD:	For making both women and men central to his plan of salvation.
OFFER THANKS:	For women whose faith has nourished yours.
CONFESS:	Any tendency to live out your own faith in a halfhearted manner, limiting the way God wants to use you.

ASK GOD: To make you unafraid of the controversy gen-
                            erated by a faithful life.

Lift Your Heart

It's a Wonderful Life is a movie that tells the heartwarming story of
George Bailey's Christmas Eve visit with an angel, who cures his sui-
cidal depression by showing him just how valuable his life has been.
The truth is, most of us have affected others in far more positive ways
than we might guess, especially if we belong to Christ. Though most
of us won't encounter an angel who tells our life story from heaven's
point of view, we can ask God for encouragement, remembering that
any good we have done has been accomplished through his grace.

Here's a simple thing you can do to help you visualize the good
effects of your faith. Consider that believers are like stones thrown into
a pond—our lives are meant to have a rippling effect so others can feel
the influence of our gifts and faith. This week, snatch a quiet moment
on your knees or in your favorite chair and close your eyes. Imagine
yourself as a stone in the hand of God. Watch him throw you out into
the water. What kind of ripples do you see? Are they large or small?
Perhaps your brother is a Christian because you shared your faith.
Maybe a child has responded to God's forgiveness because she first
experienced yours. Perhaps God has used you to bring justice to a situation of great injustice. Thank God for all the ripples your life has
already created, even if the circle of your influence still seems rather
small. Unlike the ripples created by an ordinary stone, the ripple effect
of faith need never stop as long as we live. Pray that God will make
waves with your faith, even rocking a few boats along the way.

---

*Father, I don't want to settle for the status quo, professing belief in you
and then acting as though everything good in life comes from the world
around me. Enable me to be like Priscilla, whose faith grew despite
her surroundings. Let the ripple effect of my faith build up your church.*

Women of the Bible

A One-Year Devotional Study of Women in Scripture

UPDATED AND EXPANDED

*Ann Spangler and
Jean E. Syswerda*

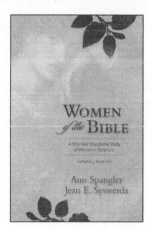

Women of the Bible focuses on fifty-two remarkable women in Scripture —women whose struggles to live with faith and courage are not unlike your own. And now this bestselling devotional study book has been updated and expanded to enhance its flexibility, usefulness, and relevance for both individuals and groups.

Small groups will especially welcome the way the Bible studies have been streamlined to fit the unique needs of the group setting. Other important changes include:

- A list of all the women of the Bible keyed to Scripture
- A timeline of the foremost women of the Bible
- A list of women in Jesus' family tree
- A list of women in Jesus' life and ministry

Vital and deeply human, the women in this book encourage you through their failures as well as their successes. You'll see how God acted in surprising and wonderful ways to draw them—and you—to himself. This year-long devotional offers a unique method to help you slow down and savor the story of God's unrelenting love for his people, offering a fresh perspective that will nourish and strengthen your personal communion with him.

Hardcover, Jacketed: 978-0-310-27055-3

*Women of Today Can Find Inspiration and Encouragement
in the Lives of the Women Who Lived in Bible Times*

Women of the Bible

52 Bible Studies for
Individuals and Groups

Jean E. Syswerda

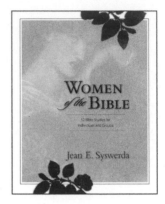

These are the inspiring stories of 52
female characters in the Bible—and
a unique resource for individuals or
groups interested in studying them
—taken from the popular book *Women of the Bible*.

*Women of the Bible: 52 Bible Studies for Individuals and
Groups* is an abridged edition of *Women of the Bible*, specifically for those who want to delve more deeply into the life of
each woman. New features include:

- the main Scripture passages that tell the story of each
  woman's life
- space for readers to record their thoughts
- a list of lesser-known women in the Bible, making this a
  complete list of all the women in the Bible
- charts and timelines

The stories of these biblical women offer encouragement
through their failures as well as through their successes. God
acted in surprising and wonderful ways in their lives, just as he
continues to act in the lives of Christian women today.

Softcover: 978-0-310-24492-9